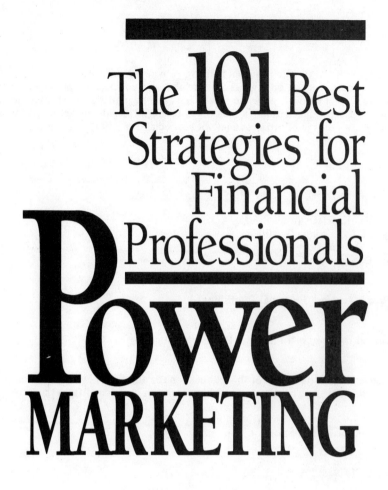

The **101** Best Strategies for Financial Professionals

Power MARKETING

Richard Wollack
& Alan Parisse

 Dearborn
Financial Publishing, Inc.

While a great deal of care has been taken to provide accurate and current information, the ideas, suggestions, general principles and conclusions presented in this book are subject to local, state and federal laws and regulations, court cases and any revisions of same. The reader is thus urged to consult legal counsel regarding any points of law—this publication should not be used as a substitute for competent legal advice.

Publisher: Kathleen A. Welton
Project Editor: Linda S. Miller
Interior Design: Lucy A. Jenkins
Cover Design: Sam Concialdi

Published by Dearborn Financial Publishing, Inc.

Printed in the United States of America.

91 92 93 10 9 8 7 6 5 4 3 2 1

Library of Congress Cataloging-in-Publication Data

Wollack, Richard G., 1945–
    Power marketing : the 101 best strategies for financial
professionals / Richard Wollack & Alan Parisse.
        p.   cm.
    Includes index.
    ISBN 0-79310-083-2 : $29.95
        1. Financial planners—Marketing.   2. Financial planners—United
States—Marketing.   I. Parisse, Alan.   II. Title.
HG179.5.W65   1990
332.6' 2—dc20
                                                        90–14046
                                                          CIP

Contents

Preface

The ideas and strategies contained in this book were assembled to provide financial professionals with a practical, easy-to-read guide of sound marketing tips and techniques. The framework for the strategies had its origin in the belief that marketing is a multifaceted and all-inclusive process extending into and even beyond each aspect of the business practice—our concept of a "marketing gestalt."

Because we believe that marketing a service and delivering that service are necessarily intertwined, many of the strategies are designed not just to increase business, but, *even more fundamentally,* to enhance the delivery of the service itself. After all, the ultimate measure of a financial adviser's success isn't how prosperous he or she is, but the degree to which the client prospers as a result of the relationship.

Why the big need for marketing in the financial industry? Historically, financial firms and practitioners have been good at selling, but not at marketing. It's not uncommon, for a new sales professional simply to be handed a list of country club members so he or she can just start dialing the numbers. That's sales, but where's the marketing?

Moreover, studies have shown that at least one out of every three financial professionals starting out in an individual practice won't make it. Competition is increasing—from independent financial professionals, as well as from major companies including brokerage firms, department stores, banks, savings and loans, and even accounting and law firms. Competition can be fierce—unless you carefully define your market and successfully communicate your value to that market. A well-thought-out approach to marketing can make the difference between struggling to survive and achieving enormous success.

This book is about identifying the specific client market in which you can be the dominant force, communicating the value and importance of your services and distinguishing yourself from the competition. We're asking you to approach the marketing challenge from every vantage point, using proven techniques that range from direct mail and public relations to "high-touch" client fulfillment—sometimes with an interesting and unusual twist. The strategies will often encourage you to be unique, to break out of the mold and establish your own special niche. Your individuality will provide the key ingredient in positioning yourself in a class apart from your competition.

Finally, take a long-term view to marketing your practice. Short-term pressures demand attention, but a few hours spent planning for the future can make all the difference for you and your clients. In the United States, our tendency is to limit ourselves to a short-term perspective. Think long-term; set your sights well into the future.

Our book owes its existence to several sources. We began by mining our own 40-plus years of combined experience observing the most successful practitioners in the financial services industries. Then, through a mix of surveys, questionnaires and interviews, we polled thousands of professionals in financial planning and related financial services across the country to glean their best marketing ideas. These contributors are listed in the "*Power Marketing* Strategy Contributors" section at the end of this book, and we would like to thank all of them for their valuable input.

We would also like to thank the staff of Dearborn Financial Publishing for their editorial contributions to this book. Finally, someone once said that "ideas are a dime a dozen. It's the person who implements them who's the real hero." In our case, the real hero is Sarah Bulgatz, whose talent and diligence made it all happen.

The strategies in this book are united by a common directive: to empower you to reach your market, promote your product and deliver impeccable, unique service that keeps clients coming back and brings in as many new ones as you're willing to serve.

Introduction

If a man can write a better book, preach a better sermon, or make a better mousetrap than his neighbor, though he builds his house in the woods the world will make a beaten path to his door.—*Ralph Waldo Emerson*

Although there may have been some truth to this saying in Emerson's time, in today's competitive marketplace you must beat a path to your *customer's* door. Stunning innovations, great products and wonderful service all mean nothing without marketing.

But even in Emerson's era, there was a significant need for marketing. In 1868, the inveterate tinkerer C.L. Sholes received the patent for the first practical typewriter. The end of the war between the states had left arms manufacturers in a desperate search for new products. In 1872, Eliphalet Remington & Sons, a firm of gunsmiths, agreed to manufacture at least 1,000 of the new machines at $125 per machine. No one quite knew who would buy Remington's typewriters, but since they dramatically increased writing speed, it was thought that scholars and theologians would provide the most likely market. Unfortunately, this did not occur, and by 1880 the firm was nearing bankruptcy. Then Remington awoke to the possibilities of the business sector, where the typewriter would allow an office worker to accomplish as many as 20 hours worth of work in one hour. Within six years, almost every sizable office had at least one typist, and the novelty of the typewriter had become a necessity. The point is that the world had always needed the typewriter; but the need wasn't recognized until it was pointed out. Without Remington's well-targeted marketing efforts, the typewriter might have sat around unused for many more years, and the firm might have gone cut of business, allowing a competitor the opportunity to develop and market the same type of product. It was well-targeted marketing that gave the Remington typewriter its context, its meaning, its value. . . and its profitability.

If you're not reaching the appropriate market—if you're not adequately describing and promoting your services—your services will lack context, meaning and value. Those services may be the best in the business, but they're of little value if no one perceives the need for them or knows how to find them.

MARKETING REDEFINED

Management guru Peter Drucker has said, "The aim of marketing is to know and understand your client so well that the product or service you offer literally sells itself." We strongly believe this statement! You need to translate that knowledge and understanding of your client (and prospect) into a way of indelibly communicating with them.

The essential objective of any marketing plan is to make the final sales process easy, or even unnecessary. All too often, marketing functions are passed along to salespeople. Although prospecting is most efficient when part of an integrated marketing program, many securities firms, for example, leave this job to sales reps. While many of the readers of this book will not be in a position to completely change the way they (or their firms) market their services, they will nonetheless obtain from this book the tools and techniques to effectively use their own marketing and sales skills.

Certain consumer products have been marketed so well that they no longer have to be "sold." Personal hygiene products provide a prime example. Not that many years ago, when water had to be carried into the house from a well, by the bucketful, most people didn't feel a need to bathe every day. But in our modern times, most of us shower at least once a day. Part of the reason is the availability of modern plumbing, but part is marketing. Before we run out of soap, we run to the store to buy more; no salesman need ever call. It's not that way with financial products and services. Important as they are to a family's future, financial products must be sold. But when the products are marketed *well,* they don't have to be sold quite as much. F.W. Woolworth, innovator and tycoon of the five-and-dime, summed it up in 1888 when he said, "I'm the world's worst salesman; therefore, I must make it easy for people to buy."

THREE TIERS TO MARKETING SUCCESS

Marketing is a three-tiered process. First, it involves finding the right prospective clients for your specific capabilities (or expanding your capabilities to match the needs of a particular group of prospective clients). Second, it involves reaching that market as efficiently as possible and communicating the value of your services to it. Finally, in today's competitive world, marketing requires delivering and promoting your service uniquely—with your own special flair—because standing out in the crowd isn't only fun, it's an essential ingredient of success. A well-executed financial program will enable you to do the following:

- Identify and research the needs of your target market(s).
- Develop a system for obtaining an extensive list and continuing influx of qualified leads.
- Promote name recognition and opportunities for client/prospect interaction.
- Establish credibility and build rapport with your clients and prospects.
- Provide superior ongoing service for optimal client retention and new client referral.

Marketing is an ongoing process, a process that many professionals tend to lose sight of as they get busy with client fulfillment. It takes time and a commitment for the long term to promote growth during good times and survival in hard times. Many of us have experienced how easy it is to ride a bicycle downhill; at that moment, we often imagine that we're great athletes. But when the road heads uphill, the picture changes. So too with client fulfillment and marketing. Creativity tends to wane when times get tough. This book will help accelerate your progress in good times, but don't forget to take it down from the shelf and reread it during the tough times as well.

Consider the time and energy that you devote to marketing as work done for your clients *in advance of getting the clients.* Just as you serve your existing clientele, your marketing activities will service your future clients. Marketing should become a part of your daily routine, just like the ongoing client service you provide. Scheduling some marketing into each work day will ensure that you don't neglect this essential component of your business activities.

The success that you ultimately achieve depends on how well you perform in three key areas: the choice of your product, the selection of your market and the ongoing promotion to your market. Each of these areas is interdependent; you must succeed in all of them to achieve overall marketing success.

MAXIMIZING RESULTS WITH THIS BOOK

We structured *Power Marketing* much like a funnel, beginning with the broad directive of market targeting and moving on within that context to the more specific directives of reaching and serving the market selected. Each of the book's eight chapters is designed to build on its predecessor and further refine and clarify your marketing focus.

We begin at the most natural and important point of departure— with an analysis of the ways in which you can identify or redefine the product you have to offer and the market that best suits your talents and objectives. From there, idea after idea will lead you through a broad spectrum of marketing tools and techniques designed, first, to help you develop a powerful prospecting list and, then, to reach those prospects. We'd like to suggest that after reading each chapter, you take a few moments to identify the strategies you'd like to try and make notes on possible variations. At the end of each chapter, you'll find an implementation plan—a checklist we've included to help you get started and get the momentum going.

Consider reading the book slowly over a period of time, perhaps only a chapter a week. Don't try to digest too much at once, because the strategies are meant to be assimilated individually; each of them, after all, has achieved success in the past. When you drive along a country road, unless you drive slowly enough, you can't distinguish the landscape's special nuances; colors and shapes merge into one another, appearing as just one nondescript blur. So it is with the ideas in the book. It's best to read just a few at time.

Some of the financial professionals reading this book will already be satisfied with their business results. They may simply be looking for a few additional ways to generate new clients. Other readers, however, may wish to see their businesses grow and evolve. Accordingly, we created the book with two distinct levels of use in mind. Within the first level, you'll find an abundance of what we call "add-on" strategies. These are designed for a quick fix—strategies that you can simply pick up and immediately put to work. They're easy to implement and soon to see results. We hope you'll try all of them.

The second level, however, may require a fundamental change in marketing perspective and philosophy. As you read through the book, you'll discover that we continually urge you to take a long-term view, to test your imagination and, perhaps, to even defer some short-term results. Incorporating this approach into your marketing philosophy can separate you from your competition and become the solid foundation for your success.

It's our hope that many of the strategies will kindle a spark and get your own creative wheels turning. Some are very specific and may not exactly suit your particular circumstances, but you'll find that they lend themselves to personalization through different twists and adaptations. Some may overlap; others may even seem to conflict. For instance, many of the ideas call for spending money, while others call for paring costs down.

Besides the 101 strategies, we have also included sub-strategies, which are denoted with an $\boxed{\text{S}}$. These are different ways of executing the larger strategies.

The use and timing of particular strategies will depend to a great extent on your individual situation, your current and desired client mix and the immediate and changing demands of the economy and your market area. Also, before using any of the ideas, you may find it appropriate to consult your firm's legal counsel or your personal attorney to ensure that you're in compliance with applicable laws and regulations.

The important thing is to evaluate the strategies. Take a look at them; find what's useful, and adapt that portion that will work for your business practice. The ideas should lead to many other evolutions of new additional ideas. But, in fact, that's what ideas are all about—stimulating the creative process.

We've purposely kept the idea descriptions as brief as possible. Our real goal for the book is to excite your imagination, to motivate you to hang your own special, unique strategies on the framework we're providing.

Remember, experimentation is often the only way to test an idea, and, most important, if one strategy doesn't suit your needs, you've got more than 100 others to try.

PART 1

The Tools for Prospecting

1 *Targeting Your Market*

A business sage once said, "At least half of all my advertising dollars are wasted. The problem is, I don't know which half." Probably the single most important concept in this book involves properly targeting your market. The "shotgun" approach, in which you market to *everyone* in the hope that someone will respond, doesn't work very well. This is particularly true in marketing financial services, primarily because of the competition that exists among financial professionals. One good way to get beyond the competition, and to stay there, is to find a specific target market (or markets) to which you can direct your marketing energy. It's important to realize that if you're marketing to everyone, you're marketing to no one.

Even if you want to be a "generalist" in your profession, you should still identify and focus on a specific target group or groups that need a generalist, groups with which you want to do business, that you believe you can serve well, and from which you'll be able to obtain viable referrals. If you run a small business, it's particularly important to target effectively because you have limited resources with which to reach clients who will become economically productive for you.

If you don't use any other idea in this book, if you do nothing else in your marketing efforts, carefully target your market to maximize your efforts and save money and time. This step in your marketing plan may not prove to be quite as much fun as some of the other strategies you'll find throughout the book, because it requires planning and may not yield immediate results. But, remember, a good marketing plan is a long-term marketing plan.

Successful targeting will make all the other steps in your marketing plan easy, providing you with a prewritten program to follow. Having a target market organizes your entire marketing focus: It means knowing exactly whom you want to meet, which newspapers and journals to read, with whom to have lunch, what to wear, which seminars and special events to attend, and maybe even what kind of car to drive (you wouldn't, for instance, call on an American auto workers' union in a foreign car). In essence, being well-targeted translates into having a purpose and a specific agenda to follow when you wake up every morning.

DEFINING YOUR PRODUCT

Ferraris and Chevrolets are both cars, but the similarity ends there. People don't simply buy cars; they buy a combination of qualities that include performance, luxury, convenience, economy, reliability, image and style. Market segments for cars consist of individuals who assign different premium values to different mixes of these qualities. For example, even if everyone could afford a Ferrari, not everyone would want one. Not everyone wants the ability to cruise at 130 miles per hour. More to the point, not everyone wants a "showy" car that can be hard to service, expensive to insure and risky to park on the street. Ferraris appeal to a select market segment that can afford to pay many times the cost of the average Chevrolet and that places a high premium on luxury, style and performance. By contrast, the individual who buys a Chevy is likely to place a higher premium on price, comfort and ease of repair. Not surprisingly, both markets have great profit potential.

Obviously, Ferraris and Chevrolets aren't the only choices a consumer has; a wide variety of automobile options exists to satisfy the demands and needs of different market segments. As you define your own product (and by "product," we mean the range and caliber of services and amenities your business offers its clientele), the question you should ask yourself is this: Are you a Ferrari, a Chevrolet or something in between?

The point is that if you're just telling the world that you're a good car, few will want to buy you. By specifically defining your product, you'll be able to more easily identify those people to whom your services appeal, and you will know how to best market those services to them.

Marketing builds credibility within the consumer groups that are interested in your product. Consumers tend to buy name brands over generics because they have faith in the name brands. Even though two products may be identical in form and composition, most consumers will opt for the name brand. For instance, the Bayer aspirin company worked hard to create its own powerful marketing aura—consisting of stability, longevity and concern, as well as analgesic expertise. Many would argue that "aspirin is aspirin," and, chemically, that's true. It's the marketing aura the company has created that makes Bayer "the most trusted name in pain relievers" and that allows the company to charge top dollar for its product. When a consumer reaches for the Bayer aspirin on the drugstore shelf, he or she has chosen to buy the image of Bayer's trustworthiness as much as the aspirin itself.

As a financial professional, your product also consists of a lot more than just the particular financial service, advice or investments you provide. It's *everything* you have to offer your clientele: the convenience of your location, the ambience of your offices, the courtesy of your staff, your accessibility and responsiveness to your clients' needs, your willingness to provide "extras." All of these factors have an enormous impact on where a potential client decides to do business (and to continue to do business). Do you, for instance, consider yourself a full-service operation, or do you see yourself as more like a "discount" brokerage firm that offers minimal service at a reduced cost? The type of product you offer will often determine the way you market it and the price you charge.

IDENTIFYING YOUR MARKET—TWO APPROACHES

Your existing or potential skills will determine your choice of a target market. You can select your market in one of two ways. The first method involves basing your choice on your own existing skills and capabilities—i.e., choosing your market according to which type of potential clients will respond best to the "product" you already have. Alternatively, you can select a market that may appeal to you and adapt or expand your product to meet its needs. Manufacturing companies do this all the time based on their studies of different markets whose needs for utility, style, quality, convenience and comfort vary. Financial professionals are really no different.

The geographical area in which you operate your business may, for example, offer a sizable market for pension plans, or for disability insurance, but you may not have the requisite skills to break into it. Develop them! Educate yourself and seek formal education to learn everything there is to know about pension plans or disability insurance. Create your product to fill market demand.

Rather than compete with the bulk of the other professionals in your market who don't have a specific target, try to identify a second, third or fourth ladder that you can climb. Consider your own professional and personal strengths and weaknesses as you focus on a market that's suited to your experience and abilities. Choosing a market requires a simultaneous process of evaluating your own skills and potential and the needs of the market that appeals to you. Developing an intimate understanding of your target market's needs is crucial to your selection and will ultimately serve your prospective clients, and you, best.

The volume of potential competition should influence your choice of a target. If a substantial amount of competition exists in a given market, your share of the market will necessarily be small. For example, even though a particular market segment may contain a great deal of wealth, if too many professionals are competing for it, none of them will do particularly well. You will likely fare better in a $500 million market where you have five competitors than in a $1 billion market where there are 20.

The most obvious way to preselect a market is by income level or net worth. For this type of targeting approach, you typically need to find clients who have money to make money. But finding wealthy clients is only one way to make your business grow.

A good practice in market targeting is to identify a group for which you have some empathy. For instance, a dentist leaving the practice of dentistry to begin a career as a financial adviser might do well to market his or her services to dentists and other medical professionals. The former dentist would have a built-in understanding of the financial needs and goals of the other medical professionals, and it would be a logical move to market to them. The same holds true for other professions as well. If, for instance, you taught school at one time, you could market your services to schoolteachers; you would understand their needs and know how to best communicate with them (see Strategy 4).

Similarly, you might have a particular interest in helping people who are undergoing transitions or major life-style changes. It may be that you yourself have had a comparable experience, or you may have other reasons for believing that you can relate especially well to them.

For example, a significant need for financial counseling arises during the divorce process. A few years ago, a California couple we knew filed for a divorce, and the wife wanted to keep the house. The already twice-divorced husband readily agreed in favor of retaining for himself the couple's multifamily rental property in San Francisco. In less than two years, the ex-wife could no longer make the payments due on the adjustable rate mortgage and had to sell the home and pay a substantial tax on what was, in fact, the couple's gain. Meanwhile, the ex-husband was earning extra income from his rental property. Clearly, the woman would have benefited from sound financial guidance before the divorce settlement was finalized. Such individuals can easily provide an entire market unto itself—one in which a financial adviser can make a meaningful contribution and, at the same time, reap substantial economic rewards.

We can extend the empathetic approach to target marketing even further. As one example, perhaps you don't like to wear business clothes and are much more comfortable in casual dress. Arguably, you should put your preference aside and play by the "rules." But another strategy would be to make the most of your preference. You might consider targeting at least some potential clients who would appreciate, and relate to, your choice of apparel because that's the way they're dressed themselves. You could, for example, market your services to health and sports club owners, or to marina owners or professional athletes—to any group that makes a profession out of recreation.

The target market you select will most likely contain numerous subtargets too. For example, suppose that you targeted clients in Westchester County, New York, who had incomes of at least $75,000 per year. Within that market, you would encounter clients over 70 years old and clients whose incomes exceeded $150,000. Your approach to these sub-groups would probably be somewhat different from your approach to the parent target group.

The essential thing to remember is to focus your marketing efforts on the target markets in which you are most likely to succeed. Think about what your services are and who the people are who will benefit from them. Consider whom you'd enjoy serving the most and whom you would serve the best. Paying attention to these strategies will ensure that the marketing dollars and time you spend will be invested wisely and productively. If you don't know where you're going, any road will take you there. When you have a specific destination in mind, it's easy to chart an appropriate course to reach it.

In summary, targeting is valuable because it enables you to focus your energy on the area that will be most productive for you, and your prospects and clients will respond better to you because they will see you as a professional with a specific interest and expertise in meeting their needs.

---

1   DESCRIBE YOUR PRODUCT

We recommend the full-service approach to the investment business. To us, however, the term "full-service" means delivering completely on the service that your product definition promises. For instance, if you define your product as meeting *all* of your client's financial needs, then you should deliver that service fully. Obviously, taking care of all of your clients' financial requirements is a route that may not work for everyone and gets tougher as the products and competition proliferate. Hence, more limited product definitions may be more valid and profitable. For example, to be successful, a discount brokerage firm need only deliver fully on whatever service it promises. Even a limited-product firm like a discount brokerage, however, still needs to offer its clients responsive, courteous attention when they call, communicating clearly the message that the firm wants to keep its clients satisfied.

To create a full-service product approach, take a look at all the services you can provide compared to all the services your clients need. You can begin by making a written list of the services your target market needs, which of them you provide and where your clients can obtain the rest. (Use the work sheet at the end of this chapter for this exercise.) You'll find that in cases where you don't provide a service directly, you may be able to offer it on a consulting basis or arrange to provide it through another financial professional.

[S] *Creating a slogan.* Don Connelly of the Putnam Companies promulgates this idea: Develop a series of slogans that quickly identify the primary benefit you provide each of your target markets. To do this, think of what you would say at a cocktail party to someone who asks what you do. Most of us would respond by saying, "I'm a stockbroker/insurance agent/financial planner," etc. But you can offer a more descriptive, effective response, such as the following:

- "I give people confidence that they'll have a comfortable retirement."

- "I help people fund their children's college educations while they maintain their current life-styles."
- "I make understanding money easy."

The objective is to develop a way of communicating the value of your services so that the person you're talking to responds by saying, "Oh, really? I need that!"

Think about how you would describe what you do to a 40-year-old couple, a 75-year-old retiree, a single mother, a medical doctor, an accountant or an investment banker. What type of slogans can you create for your market(s)?

S *Identifying your features and benefits.* To describe your product, think about your personal and professional features and benefits and how they might translate into client benefits. The following type of work sheet is designed to help you define and clarify your own personal and professional appeal to the target market(s) you select. As you complete your own work sheet, pay particular attention to any "lemons" that may be present in your features and benefits showcase. For example, if you are young and marketing to older people, your age might be perceived as a negative. You can, however, look for ways to turn this lemon into lemonade. Granted, youth may imply inexperience, but it can also mean recent education, high energy and enthusiasm. You should identify these positive qualities and emphasize them.

Sample Features and Benefits Work Sheet

Your Features and Benefits

	Features	Benefits to the Client
Age/experience	_____	_____
Current work	_____	_____
Previous work	_____	_____
Formal education	_____	_____
Expertise or focus	_____	_____
Personal traits	_____	_____
Hobbies, interests	_____	_____
"Lemons"	_____	_____
Other	_____	_____

Your Firm's Features and Benefits

	Features	Benefits to the Client
Size	_____	_____
Specialty	_____	_____
Philosophy	_____	_____
Other	_____	_____
	_____	_____
	_____	_____

Now carefully choose the few words that best describe your product. (If you have more than one product, identify a few key words for each product.) After you've made your selection, think about how the words you've selected might be adapted into a phrase or slogan that you could use to describe to others what you do. The following provides an example.

Product 1: General Financial Planning Services	Product 2: Asset Allocation	Product 3: Pension Specialization
1. Creative	Intelligent	Goal-oriented
2. Imaginative	Researched	Strategic
3. Balanced	Timely	Responsive
4. Responsive	Targeted	Detail-oriented
5. Mature	Balanced	Timely
6. Long-term	Diversified	Prudent

Target Market 1
  Slogan: Imaginative solutions to long-term investor needs
Target Market 2
  Slogan: Intelligent, targeted advice for diversifying portfolios
Target Market 3
  Slogan: Prudent, timely advice for achieving strategic goals

STRATEGY

2   Target Your Market by Financial Status

Financial status provides one of the most obvious approaches to market segmentation. It can be helpful to describe the overall market as consisting of four different tiers (Figure 1–1):

Tier I: **The product purchase market**—primarily blue-collar workers who have little, if any, disposable income, and minimal net worth. Family income levels satisfy the basic needs for subsistence, with little extra. The financial requirements of this group are specifically related to particular products—insurance, for instance, or mutual funds for IRAs. In a sense, the product does the planning.

Tier II: **The directive planning market**—middle-income families with annual incomes of approximately $40,000 to $80,000 and modest net worths (mostly in home equity). Financial counseling parameters are basic and generally straightforward; the emphasis is on optimizing the standard of living through saving and diversified investment.

Figure 1–1.   The Four Market Tiers

Tier IV:
_____
Wealthy ($250,000 +)

Tier III:
_____
Middle- to upper-level ($100,000 +)

Tier II:
_____
Middle-income families ($40,000 to $80,000 +)

Tier I:
_____
Blue-collar workers (Below $40,000)

Appropriate products include insurance, IRAs, mutual funds and perhaps a selective investment in individual stocks or a limited partnership.

Tier III: The sophisticated market—small business owners, middle- to upper-level corporate managers, professionals and executives who generally earn at least $100,000 per annum and up to $250,000 and who have moderate to substantial net worths. Financial needs include sophisticated planning and diverse products. Occasionally, unique product solutions are required. A financial adviser has the opportunity within this market tier to help establish meaningful estate growth.

Tier IV: The leadership market—the wealthy, with net worths in excess of $1 million and those earning $250,000 per annum and higher. Services targeted to this market segment often revolve around maintaining safety of principal, current tax and estate planning, and meeting a more diverse set of financial objectives. Servicing the leadership market also requires a coordinated effort among all the relevant financial professionals involved, such as accountants, attorneys, trust officers and other financial advisers such as insurance agents and stock brokers. Within this tier, the need for unique and attractive product solutions is high.

If you're an experienced and sophisticated practitioner, you should probably aim high. Specifically, it will often pay to direct your marketing efforts toward tiers III and IV. After all, that's where *you*—more than the investment product—will make a difference. Also, to maximize your income, it generally works best to serve clients who have high incomes or high net worths. Perhaps it's obvious, but all too often, financial professionals spend too much time in the bottom two tiers (I and II) and not enough in the top two.

If you decide to focus on the top tiers, you must make the commitment to direct your marketing efforts primarily to them. Moreover, if you focus on an upscale market, accepting clients who don't have the financial characteristics you've targeted will eat into your time and divert you from your target. Additionally, if you focus on an upscale market, over time your style, approach and expertise will become such that you will not be particularly adept at understanding and fulfilling the needs of lower-income clients. Be aware that the opposite also holds true. If you target the lower end, you probably won't be able to fully satisfy the needs of the upper end as well.

Are you afraid that you won't be able to find enough tier III and IV clients? It may be a problem in some rural areas of the United States, but not in most metropolitan centers.

Approximately 1.4 million millionaires live in the United States, based on U.S. Department of Commerce data. Let's suppose that you live in the San Francisco Bay Area. The population of the San Francisco Bay Area comprises about two percent of the national population. If we apply that percentage to the number of millionaires in the country, we can estimate that San Francisco and its environs contain roughly 28,000 millionaires. Some of those millionaires probably have net worths of $100 million; others have $50 million; still others have $5 million. To be conservative, let's just say that the average millionaire in the Bay Area has $2 million. Multiply that estimated average net worth by the number of San Francisco Bay Area millionaires, and the result is $56 billion dollars! What these numbers demonstrate is the existence of a substantial need for financial planning services and products. So if you want high-income clients, market to them—and to them only. You should be able to find plenty of them out there.

By the way, if your market area has fewer wealthy people than the San Francisco Bay Area, it probably also contains fewer competing financial professionals. In fact, you'll probably find that the ratio of wealthy individuals to financial professionals is disproportionately more favorable in smaller markets.

How can you target tier III and IV clients? Here's just one example. Joseph C. Bowers, a financial planner with Financial Advisory Network in Radnor, Pennsylvania, has combined his political interests with his marketing strategy by serving as a finance chairman for a Senate re-election committee. This connection has provided him a tremendous opportunity to market his own services to both tier III and IV prospects who are invited to attend fund-raisers. Chapter 2— "Developing A Data Base of Prospects"—will give you additional specific tips on how to develop a prospecting list of well-to-do individuals.

Be aware, however, that the market you select may contain some millionaires who aren't wealthy. Does that sound like a paradox? It isn't. Consider the couple of modest means who bought a house 30 years ago in what would later become a very desirable area and now sit on more than $1 million in real estate equity. Or, consider the family that owns your neighborhood dry cleaning store. They too may very well be sitting on substantial business equity. Even the 40-year-old mechanic who owns and operates the successful foreign car service garage may be a secret millionaire. This, in fact, is a market that has a great need for professional planning services and may be one that you choose to target.

Although wealthy individuals often provide the most lucrative market segment, there's money to be made and a valuable service to be provided to the middle-income market in tier II, the directive planning market. Middle-income people usually have a smaller tolerance for error in making investment decisions and thus have a significant need for financial and estate planning assistance. In marketing to tier II prospects, you'll find that your business will be most profitable if you work toward using lower-cost associates and assistants to service your clientele. The work is relatively simpler; you'll find that you probably won't need to do it all yourself and that a higher client volume could be more profitable for you.

It's very difficult to successfully work with tier I because of the very high volume of clients needed to generate a profit. We feel that tier I is best left to the generic financial services providers such as banks, savings and loans and other large mass service providers that are set up expressly to handle the larger volumes.

Of course, you may choose to spend some time working with tier I clients in order to actively integrate your personal socioeconomic concerns into your business practice. Many financial professionals have discovered that this proves extremely rewarding on both a personal and professional level. We don't recommend, however, making tier I your exclusive target market; it's tough to make a living from it.

⑤ *Targeting your market by investment objective.* Aggressive growth, speculation, equity appreciation, safety of principal, current income: All these and many more are valid investment objectives. While assets may be allocated among individual investment vehicles with different objectives, at the extremes clients tend to have different styles, needs and concerns. Therefore, another way of targeting your market is by risk tolerance.

You may feel more comfortable working with aggressive-growth investors who are willing to take big risks to get big returns, or you may prefer working with more conservative investors who have safety of principal as their primary objective. If you take the "boom or bust" route, targeting individuals who are high-rollers, your business will probably follow the same boom and bust cycles that have an impact on your clients' investments. While this can be very exciting, it necessitates careful planning to accommodate the business slumps you're likely to experience. Targeting high-rollers usually means that you'll also need to keep prospecting for new clients due to the higher level of client burnout that almost always accompanies higher-risk investment. Conversely, if you select a more conservative type of investor as your target market, chances are you'll be able to establish a more stable client base.

STRATEGY

3   TARGET YOUR MARKET BY AGE OR SOCIAL GROUP

Seniors, for instance, age 55 and older, are the fastest growing segment of the population and can provide a high-growth market for you to tap. Seniors often have a substantial amount of money to invest, which should be increasing in the 1990s as the first IRA investments begin to reach maturity and the time of potential withdrawal. Geography is important in determining the number of seniors who have investible assets. Florida, for example, where many people retire, contains nearly three times as many millionaires as California. The American Association of Retired Persons (AARP) might have a chapter in your area, which you could contact in order to offer to do a seminar or perhaps a mailing of some free information to chapter members.

People generally are living longer, and this increasing longevity is creating an entirely new set of financial requirements and necessities— particularly for middle-income, tier II, individuals. The structure of nuclear families has changed such that all the members of a family don't necessarily live together, and outside assistance is often needed to help care for older relatives who live alone. All too often, old age proves to be the worst time in a person's life, a stressful time when a caring financial professional can make a meaningful contribution. As an example, high medical costs can completely destroy a family's financial base; a family with a nest egg of $250,000 to $300,000 can't continue to pay unreimbursed medical expenses for very long without unraveling an entire lifetime of saving. The poor can immediately qualify for Medicaid; the wealthy can afford to pay for their own medical costs; middle-income people, however, are the hardest hit. You can target middle-income families to help them plan for the costs of extended medical care without shattering their life savings. In this arena, as a financial professional, you have the opportunity to do a tremendous amount of good—especially if you get people to start planning early.

S *Background.* It may be that your best market will consist of people who are in a socioeconomic class comparable to yours, who have a similar educational background, or who are in your approximate age group. People often feel most comfortable when they are around others who are like them. Because mutual confidence and trust are key to the relationships you build with your clientele, selecting a target market with which you have characteristics, qualities and interests in common will go a long way toward fostering good relationships.

S *Gender.* Gender too may provide a targeting opportunity in certain circumstances. For example, some women who are financial professionals target other women as their clients. These professionals feel that a special connection and empathy often exist, that it's easier for some women to do business with other women and that, in fact, they themselves might prefer to do business with other women.

Kathleen Muldoon, a certified financial planner (CFP) with Carter Financial Management in Dallas, Texas, devotes approximately one-third of her business to divorce planning for women. Believing that a woman going through the divorce process very often feels more comfortable working through the details of a financial settlement with another woman than with a man, and being very willing herself to spend a lot of "hand-holding" time with her clients, she began seeking referrals from local divorce attorneys with whom she had worked. All of her divorce-related business has arisen from referrals from satisfied clients and from divorce attorneys to whom she has marketed her services.

S *Other affinity groups.* People with common roots often relate very well to one another. They often embrace each other's ideas more quickly and even trust each other more than they would a person from outside their ethnic group. All else being equal, people with common roots will probably respond better to you, with your familiar background, than they will to another financial professional with similar qualifications but different background.

It's simply good marketing to target "affinity" groups with which you feel comfortable and that feel comfortable with you. Affinity groups come in many different varieties and do not necessarily have to involve ethnic background. The group with which you feel affinity can be a group that has the same religious commitments, political bent, geographic dispersion or even hobbies. One stockbroker, a transplanted

East Coast southerner living in northern California, targets other ex-patriot southerners. More than a few ex-New Yorkers do the same. The important thing is to find the group with which you have the potential to develop and sustain the strongest bond.

4   TARGET YOUR MARKET BY CLIENT PROFESSION

This can be an effective strategy, particularly if your practice is located in an area of high density for that profession. You could, for instance, market your services primarily to one or two of the following categories:

- Physicians
- Dentists
- Architects
- Teachers
- Engineers
- Attorneys
- CPAs
- Graphic designers
- Airline pilots
- Corporate executives
- Real estate agents
- Restaurateurs
- Entertainers
- Athletes

CPAs and attorneys can make a great target market, first, because they are relatively sophisticated and, second, because they can also bring in a lot of new business by referring their own clients to you.

But just as you advise your clients to diversify their investment portfolios, you should have more than one client target. If, for instance, you target real estate owners or agents and the economy suffers a depression, you'll find yourself in trouble unless you have alternative or secondary target clients.

⑤ *Small business owners.* A group to which you may be able to relate well is small business owners. As an independent practitioner, you've had personal experience in setting up your own shop and thus have an innate understanding of the small business owner's financial concerns.*

For Lewis Walker, an Atlanta-based financial planner, investment adviser and entrepreneur, the key to success is what he calls "the business of business." Seeing a wealth of opportunity in small to mid-size businesses, Walker has made them his target. He builds trust by becoming a valued financial adviser to his clients and in that way opens a second door to the possibility of integrating personal financial planning, estate planning and asset management services with the business and international expansion consulting services he provides.

"The trick," explains Walker, "is just *getting* to the business owner because there are a lot of ways in which you can provide valuable services to small and mid-sized firms. A great door-opener is simply to ask the business owner a question as obvious as, 'Do you know what your business is worth?' It's surprising how many of them don't." This usually leads to a discussion concerning the owner's ultimate goals for disposition of his or her closely held business interest and ideas relative to management succession and estate planning.

Walker carries two different business cards. One card identifies him as a CFP with Walker Capital Management Corporation, a registered investment advisory firm whose primary focus is on asset management. His second card identifies him as president of Sterling Westminster International, an international financial consulting firm with headquarters in Atlanta and offices in London, helping successful U.S. businesses expand into the European market.

His involvement with Sterling Westminster is the expression of Walker's lifelong fascination with international affairs and travel. The consulting he does as a Sterling principal has provided him the means

---

*To stay in touch with the needs and concerns of small to mid-sized business owners, try subscribing to *Small Business Reports*, a monthly newsletter that contains a selection of valuable information culled from approximately 250 nationwide business-oriented publications. It might give you useful ideas for your own business and for passing along to your clients. The periodical is published by Business Research and Communications in Monterey, California. Subscriptions are $100 per year, available by phoning 1-800-525-0643.

by which he is able to integrate his personal interests with his day-to-day work.

Walker's experience taught him that success in international business largely depends on meeting the right people and gaining their trust. Key to doing business overseas is the practice of obtaining proper introductions from businesspeople of respected position. Accordingly, Sterling Westminster offers a unique service for the business entrepreneur seeking help in international expansion. Using London as a base, this service brings the entrepreneur into Europe as an insider who is supported by an extensive network of resources and facilities. Participants in the service benefit by receiving the specific direction, knowledge, introductions and contacts that are key to success in the European business arena. They also receive extensive assistance in obtaining licenses, executing business agreements and establishing offices or other facilities when they need a more permanent location than that already provided for their use by Sterling Westminster.

As a business consultant and adviser, and in concert with an established network of resources, Walker offers his clientele other services as well:

- Helping write a comprehensive business plan.
- Raising venture capital—Large investment bankers typically aren't interested in the smaller firms that look for capital in the $1 million to $5 million range. This is a unique market niche.
- Facilitating mergers and acquisitions.

The bottom-line service that Walker provides his clients involves information management translated into action agendas. According to Walker, "The human mind can only assimilate so much at a time and 'information overload' continues to be a growing problem. For the professional adviser, this is good news. People will continue to need consultants to help them wade through, interpret and target the reams of information available. Those consultants who can deliver specific, applicable, action-oriented information will always be well received."

You might consider an indirect approach to your target group. For instance, it can often prove more fruitful to prospect to a potential client's spouse than directly to the client. As an example, a good presentation to an association of physicians' spouses may provide you with a direct line to the physicians themselves.

[s] *CPAs.* Consider this for another, perhaps more substantive, indirect approach: certified public accountants have the public's highest level of trust in providing advice on financial matters, and they are often associated with a great deal of wealth. Many CPAs are very appreciative of competent financial professionals who will work with them. Offering yourself as a valuable resource even when you don't stand to profit directly by it will often create a genuine and deserved feeling of indebtedness on the part of the CPA that will express itself in referrals for a long time to come. Three or four carefully nurtured relationships like this could very well eliminate your prospecting efforts forever.

Joe Foss, an investment planner in San Francisco, has a unique way of working with CPAs. With 20 years' experience in the investment business, he has found that working with CPAs has provided the greatest source of additional business for his firm. He markets his services primarily to CPAs and has even designed his brochure expressly to relate to their needs and concerns. His approach is to provide the CPA his services as a valuable resource who can help solve the investment planning problems of the CPA's clients. He approaches his CPA prospects in a way that doesn't detract from their working (profit-making) time, offering to present his ideas over breakfast or a brown-bag lunch.

The key, according to Foss, is making sure that the CPA recognizes that referring clients to him will essentially enable the CPA to provide better service to those clients. This is an extremely powerful motivator due to the competition among accounting firms for existing clientele. Also, the CPAs he works with are made to understand that they will only be endorsing Foss's services as an investment planner and not any investment products that he might recommend to their clients. When he makes an investment recommendation, Foss sends a letter to the CPA's client that presents the recommendation accompanied by the following disclaimer: "This investment recommendation is entirely the responsibility of Foss & Company, and it is not endorsed or approved by [the CPA firm] or [the CPA]." A copy of the letter also goes to the CPA. If the investment isn't successful, the CPA should be off the hook; conversely, if it performs well, the CPA may get accolades for his or her wisdom in referring the investment planner. Foss believes that this type of letter is an essential ingredient in encouraging CPAs to provide numerous, high-quality referrals.

5 TARGET YOUR MARKET BY FINANCIAL SERVICE OR SPECIALTY

Specialization is the specific implementation of targeting. Specializing in a particular service offers you a way to attack a market that may otherwise be unavailable because of excessive competition. But simply identifying your special market isn't enough in itself. You need to prepare yourself to offer unique services and specialized skills, matching your expertise and abilities to the market's needs. To target the pension plan market, for example, you must be knowledgeable about pension plans' funding requirements, structuring methods that maximize benefits, which investments are prohibited and which are favored, the rules governing "top heavy" plans and a lot more. It's very important to remember too that specialization is a continuous process. In pension plans, a particular investment product or strategy that's in vogue one year may fall out of favor the next. By keeping abreast of pertinent industry developments, you'll be able to continually modify and adapt your own investment approach to prevent the market from moving away from you.

Cultivating your expertise in a particular area will therefore necessitate additional education, which will further enhance your aura of professionalism. Marketing your services will become easier because specializing will make you different from your competition, and your services will be more specifically and narrowly defined. By becoming an expert and promoting your expertise, you'll easily get referrals from your existing clients and from other financial professionals as well who will come to rely on you for your specialized knowledge. And, finally, your income will grow, because specialists typically can charge more for their services than generalists.

Some potential areas and groups for specializing include the following:

[S] *Corporate employee benefit plans.* You can specialize in management of 401(k) plans, pension plans or health and education benefit plans.

⑤ *Insurance.* This can include health, disability, life, property, casualty or business insurance.

⑤ *Pre-divorce and post-divorce planning.* You can help individuals through the often difficult settlement process and establish a plan to address future financial needs.

⑤ *Disabilities.* Sudden illnesses or disabilities can wreak havoc with a family's or individual's finances. This is often the time when people need financial advice the most.

⑤ *Financial counseling for widows and widowers.* This is another opportunity to provide a valuable and much-needed service.

⑤ *Retirement and pre-retirement.* At this time, people typically come into large sums of money from corporate profit-sharing or pension plans or from other maturing investments and often seek financial guidance.

⑤ *Charitable giving.* For tier III and IV prospects in particular, this is an area of great interest.

⑤ *Living trusts.* In estate planning, living trusts appeal to individuals in all four market tiers as a means to avoid probate.

⑤ *Financial planning for corporate employees.* An employer-sponsored employee benefit such as a financial plan tends to enhance goodwill, and thus increases employee productivity, since it demonstrates that the employer truly cares about the employees' welfare. Offer your services to owners of firms with 100 or fewer employees who are well-compensated "gold-collar" professionals.

To select a specialty, first take a look at the population in your market area and determine what their needs are. Second, but equally as important, you should strive to create a match between your own interests and the needs of the market. Finally, consider your ability to reach the market in light of the marketing tools available and your competitive environment.

You don't need to give up your general practice while you're establishing yourself as a specialist. You do, of course, need to educate yourself adequately in your chosen area of specialization and to keep up-to-date on developments in both your general practice and specialty.

An easy, but important, way to begin promoting yourself as a specialist is to print an additional set of business cards, and possibly even a second brochure, that identifies and promotes your specialty, and give either of them out when it's appropriate to do so. You can also build your reputation as a specialist by speaking at seminars, workshops or conferences on topics within your area of expertise and by writing articles or being quoted in newspapers and other periodicals (see Chapter 6, strategies 68–70).

Of course, some financial professionals may not be able to invest sufficient time in additional education. You don't necessarily have to. If you're not going to become an expert in the specialty yourself, hire someone else who already is an expert in that area or subcontract the service out to the professional. This will enable you to provide your clients with the extra attention they need, furthering your image as a caring provider who can deliver special service. You must make certain, however, that you know enough about the specialty to choose the right subcontractor and to diagnose problems and identify opportunities for your clients.

6   TARGET YOUR MARKET BY PRODUCT SPECIALTY

Focus on selling a product that has a built-in special-interest group. For instance, certain investment programs have been designed to invest exclusively in marinas. Boat owners are naturally interested in programs like this. Obtain a mailing list of boat owners and do a mailing and telephone follow-up to them. Here are some other investments that might appeal to a particular market group:

- Medical building properties, medical equipment or stock in aggressive-growth biotech firms for physicians and other medical professionals
- Airport-related properties for airline pilots and personnel
- Resort properties or golf courses for avid golfers
- Business insurance for new business owners, including key executive insurance
- High-tech venture capital offerings for engineers or computer systems analysts (but watch out: they might drive you crazy evaluating your ideas!)

STRATEGY

7   GET TO KNOW YOUR TARGETS

You can get to know your prospects by researching books and studies written on your particular target group, developing and sending out your own fact-finding survey or questionnaire and by simply asking a lot of questions during client/prospect interviews. You'll typically find that research studies and surveys of your target market that include valuable statistics are available from applicable trade associations, special interest publications, newspapers and in general literature. A library search could well pay off handsomely.

⬚ *Psychological profiles.* The benefit of using this type of tool is that it allows you to improve and polish your communication with your target market; by understanding their emotional needs, you'll be able to effectively respond to all of their cues. You'll also find that it will heighten your awareness of and sensitivity to those special targets who may not conform to the norm.

The following client profile form may give you some strategies for developing your own fact-finding survey.

Client Profile Information Form

Client name: _____ Age: _____

Nickname: _____

Address: _____

   Occupation and title: _____

   Employer: _____

   Annual income (current): _____ Expected income: _____

Spouse or significant other name: _____ Age: _____

   Occupation and title: _____

   Employer: _____

   Annual income: _____

Children's names and ages: _____

_____

_____

Client's Personal Information*

Political leaning (if any): _____

Religious commitment (if any): _____

Spending style (i.e., spendthrift or saver? What does client spend the most on?): _____

_____

Investment preferences:	Investment goals:
1. _____	1. _____
2. _____	2. _____
3. _____	3. _____

What would prevent attainment of these goals? _____

Hobbies and interests: _____

Spouse's or significant other's hobbies: _____

Children's hobbies: _____

[S] *Understanding your clients' special needs.* If you target senior citizens, for instance, or just have certain clients who happen to be seniors, you can take specific steps to address their special needs:

- Invite them to bring a younger relative or friend to your meetings. It will often add to their feeling of comfort as they make decisions, and it will also ensure that they hear and remember the gist of your discussion.
- Make sure that the written information you give them is in large enough type so that they can read it.
- Make it easy for them to meet with you. (See Chapter 7, Strategy 83.)

---

*Please note that obtaining this type of personal information can allow you to provide better service to your clients by enhancing your sensitivity to their special customs and needs. For instance, if you acquired new clientele who were Mormons and you wanted to take them out to dinner, you would know not to order wine with the meal. Or if you had clients who were Seventh Day Adventists or Orthodox Jews, you would know that you shouldn't try to schedule Saturday meetings.

If you incorporate this kind of target thinking into your marketing strategy, it will demonstrate empathy and ultimately result in better service.

TO GET STARTED...

We can't emphasize strongly enough how important it is to avoid shotgun marketing. Identifying one or two specific target markets will empower you with the focus and the direction you need to obtain the productive clientele you need—and the clientele for which you'll be able to do the most good. Being well-targeted means knowing exactly how and where to spend your time and marketing dollars without waste.

You can, of course, always change your target market. The needs of the marketplace, economic conditions and your own changing abilities and preferences will help you determine when and if it's appropriate to select a different target group or groups. Bear in mind that defining your product and targeting your market are dynamic processes, ever subject to change. You should periodically evaluate and modify your product and market suitability as both you and the world around you evolve. If you've done your targeting well, there are only three reasons why you won't succeed: (1) you've chosen the wrong market, (2) you have the wrong product for the market or (3) you're not doing enough promotion.

To define your product, create a list of financial services, which your target market may need, in each case identifying the service provider and method of compensation. Use the following example as a format.

Service	Current Provider	General Compensation
Estate planning:	_____	_____
Investment planning:	_____	_____
Investment placement	_____	_____
(e.g., stocks, bonds,	_____	_____
partnerships, trusts):	_____	_____

Service	Current Provider	General Compensation
Tax planning:	_____	_____
Tax preparation:	_____	_____
Real estate (sales/acquisitions):	_____	_____
Negotiations:	_____	_____
Business planning:	_____	_____
Family business successive planning:	_____	_____
Insurance (health, life, disability, home, auto, business):	_____	_____
Other:	_____	_____
	_____	_____
	_____	_____

Now think about which of these services you can provide yourself or provide through an association with other professionals. This is an important step in targeting your market.

1. Describe your target market(s). Be as specific as possible in regard to age, income level, social group, special need, etc.
    Primary target 1: _____
        Sub-target a: _____
        Sub-target b: _____
        Sub-target c: _____
    Primary target 2: _____
        Sub-target a: _____
        Sub-target b: _____
        Sub-target c: _____
    Primary target 3: _____
        Sub-target a: _____
        Sub-target b: _____
        Sub-target c: _____

2. If you have more than one major target market, identify them in order of their priority to your business.

    _____

    _____

    _____

3. Once you've defined your target, think about what you can do to enhance your product and get closer to your potential and existing clients. Try identifying the following avenues of opportunity:
    Periodicals to follow: _____
    Books to read: _____
    Courses to take: _____
    Associations/clubs to join: _____
    Charitable or civic organizations to join: _____
    Conventions/conferences to attend: _____
    Other avenues? _____
    Should you provide additional staff training, or add to your staff?

    _____

4. What special skills do you have or can you acquire?

    _____

5. List three strategies in this chapter that you can use.
    1. _____
    2. _____
    3. _____

6. List any additional strategies—not in the book—that occurred to you as you were reading the chapter.

    _____

7. Identify two strategies you'd like to try and the steps you'll need to take to implement them.
    Strategy: _____
    (continue on next page)

Implementation   Who Will Implement
Steps: Date To Complete: the Steps If Not You?
1. _____   1. _____   1._____
2. _____   2. _____   2._____
3. _____   3. _____   3._____
4. _____   4. _____   4._____

Strategy: _____

Implementation   Who Will Implement
Steps: Date To Complete: the Steps If Not You?
1. _____   1. _____   1._____
2. _____   2. _____   2._____
3. _____   3. _____   3._____
4. _____   4. _____   4._____

8.   What do you expect to accomplish by implementing these ideas?

_____

2 *Developing a Data Base of Prospects*

Once you target a market conceptually, the next step is to identify the specific individuals or organizations that belong within it. Developing a data base of prospects is a key step, but be careful. While information is power, if it's not organized properly, it can become a burden and a competitive disadvantage.

Once you've identified your target market, you'll need to build a list of suitable individuals to whom you should market your services. Developing a list that's specific to your target market(s) will take some work, but if you spend the time and energy laying this important groundwork, the marketing steps that follow will become progressively easier. The response to your marketing efforts will be proportionate to how well you organize and develop your data base.

In essence, this chapter is about looking for leads—leads that will enable you to create a powerful prospecting list. Finding leads is different from getting referrals—that's a subject that we'll cover in Chapter 6. Building your list of leads is equivalent to building a data base, a source of information that you'll consistently use to implement your external marketing efforts.

Your prospecting list will give you a target for a variety of marketing tactics, including direct mail solicitation, cold-calling, seminar invitations and newsletter mailings. The possibilities are vast. As a data base, the list will require ongoing attention. You should update it regularly to at least reflect changes in your prospects' names or addresses.

There's no excuse for a target prospect receiving a piece of mail that contains an obsolete address, outdated business affiliation or incorrect or misspelled name; it just makes a poor impression. Updating the data base from time to time will also ensure that you eliminate prospects who have become rejects.

Depending on how detail-oriented you are, a good practice that we recommend is to make your data base work harder for you by computerizing it. Computerization will allow you to include more in-depth information:

- The source of the lead
- The date you added the lead to your list
- All of the dates on which you made contact with the prospect and the outcome of those contacts
- The standard business salutation you use with the prospect (e.g., "Dear George" or "Dear Mr. Jones")
- The types of marketing materials used
- The date of the next scheduled contact
- Any other unique information you wish to capture, such as the client's investment interests and other firms with which he or she has an account

Several software programs have these capabilities. Computer-assisted follow-up will enable you to keep track of your prospects and clients on a monthly, bimonthly or seminannual basis. You can designate the appropriate time frame that will work best for you and modify the program to include the specific tracking features you want. Depending on how sophisticated your needs are, you can also have a highly personalized program of this type written for you, although it will cost more.

Regardless of how you plan to use them, you should make a habit of continually collecting leads and expanding your data base. Even if you don't plan to use new leads right away, you'll find that you can always use them later on. In fact, you can develop primary, secondary and even tertiary lists—to be used for different marketing purposes at different times.

There are literally hundreds of ways to research leads. The following techniques are proven winners for expanding your data base.

---

⑧　TAKE ADVANTAGE OF PUBLIC RECORDS

In our open society, we have access to an extraordinary amount of "public" information, which actually contains a great deal of private data. This information can supply you with many new leads.

⑤ *Contributors to political campaigns.* You can obtain from the state the names of contributors to major political campaigns. These contain an abundance of information: In addition to the contributor's name and obvious political leanings, such lists contain the contributor's profession, home address and the amount of money contributed.

⑤ *Registered voters.* You can also go to the registrar of voters to develop a list of names and addresses from the wealthiest voting precincts in town.

⑤ *Retired/retiring school teachers.* Public school board minutes are another good source of leads; they'll provide the names of school teachers who have recently retired.

⑤ *Parents of college-bound children.* You can obtain elementary school directories and send personalized letters to the children's parents explaining the tax implications of saving for a child's higher education and offering your financial advisory services and solutions in this area.

⑤ *Tier III and IV executives.* (See Strategy 2.) Proxies from publicly traded companies list all the principals and officers of the company; how much they were paid during the year, including a summary of their options, insurance and other benefits; and the towns or cities where they live.

---

9   REVIEW NEW CHAMBERS OF COMMERCE LISTINGS

Chambers of commerce member booklets provide an excellent source of leads, particularly if your target market consists of small business owners. Most chambers of commerce also sponsor monthly "mixer" meetings that are open to the public. These can provide you with the opportunity for face-to-face introductions to some of your new prospects.

It's also possible to obtain mailing lists from chambers of commerce. These lists include all the clubs and different organizations in the area.

---

10 USE THE NEWSPRINT MEDIA

You'll find that a variety of trade publications offer a wealth of new client leads. Here are just a few ideas on which publications to use and what you can find in them.

S *Business publications that include insider trading reports.* Fay F. Jones in Menlo Park, California, looks for lists of intentions to sell publicly traded stocks to obtain the names and addresses of individuals coming into large sums of money.

S *The "business opportunities" section of* **The Wall Street Journal.** This is a hot spot for potential prospects advertising their tax-shelter, income and sales and buying needs.

S *Local newspapers.* Large real estate transactions are regularly listed in local newspapers, along with pertinent information about the terms of the sale, the buyer and the seller.

You can also find divorce notices in some local newspapers. Philip R. Walters in Orlando, Florida, takes advantage of the fact that legal files are open to the public; he selects several cases that are listed in the newspaper and then reviews all of the related documents that are filed in court, including financial declarations and property settlement agreements. He then sends a letter and brochure describing his specialized financial services to the party he believes would most benefit from his help. Often, however, sending just one letter isn't enough. Persistence gains attention. (See Strategy 40.)

Promotions and announcements in local newspapers will also tip you off to individuals who are moving into positions of prominence, wealth or other areas of target market-related interest to you.

Similarly, the obituaries provide fertile ground for developing your list of leads. If your target market consists of widows and widowers, this is a prime place to start looking for prospects who would benefit from your expertise at an important time.

11   USE NEWSLETTERS TO AUGMENT YOUR DATA BASE

Privately published newsletters often contain valuable information that can help you generate new leads.

⒮ *Alumni news.* Susan E. Arbuckle in Columbia, Maryland, looks for leads in the alumni publication from her alma mater. She finds that this works exceptionally well since she and the alumni prospects she finds already share a common bond. She identifies those individuals moving into her area and, from among them, who might become a productive client. She also looks for individuals in related fields for referrals and possible collaborative work.

⒮ *In-house corporate newsletters.* Corporate newsletters often recognize employees for length of service. You can make a practice of reading the newsletters of large local companies to identify those individuals who will soon be facing retirement.

12   HOW ABOUT A "TWOFER"?

How would you like to play more golf, tennis or racquetball? How would you like to spend more time sailing or doing more of any of the recreational activities you enjoy? Here's a way for you to do what you like to do and get leads at the same time. You can think of your recreational time as yet another opportunity to be professionally productive. Make a practice of inviting clients or potential clients to participate in the recreational activity with you. The time spent together will build strong bonds as well as be enjoyable.

Many of the people you meet at your health, sports or yacht club are also potential clients. You don't need to actively market your services to them; just being active is sufficient. You'll find that many people will be naturally drawn to you and your professional expertise because of the recreational interests that you have in common.

John Coffey in Carnegie, Pennsylvania, has essentially created his own market, which offers a ready-made data base, by starting an "over-30" baseball league in Pittsburgh. The social ties that develop in this context invariably generate new business. In fact, Coffey claims that the baseball league has been his best source of clients and referrals, in addition to being a lot of fun!

Another broker, in Chicago, takes his clients fishing for half-day and full-day excursions, inviting them to bring guests of their choosing. His boat provides a relaxed environment in which he and his clients (and prospects) talk business. He claims that almost 40 percent of his business results from his involvement in sportfishing and his participation in boating and fishing organizations.

[S] *Trying an epicurean approach.* T.R. Metzger of First Financial Group of Illinois has a novel, cost-efficient and relatively quick way of gathering a lot of leads. He sponsors free dinner-for-two drawings at the better restaurants in town. Restaurant patrons deposit their business cards in a fishbowl at the restaurant in order to qualify for the drawing. The restaurant benefits by Metzger's advance purchase of a dinner for two and the good publicity from the dinner giveaway; Metzger benefits by accumulating the business cards of numerous affluent potential leads.

---

13   SHARE LEADS

Here's a good way to generate leads. Form a group with several (seven to nine) other service and product professionals who are very successful in sales and agree to meet periodically for breakfast or lunch—perhaps once a month. Exchange names of prospects and clients with them. The group might consist of financial planners, attorneys, insurance brokers, CPAs, real estate agents, trust officers and perhaps even cellular phone salespeople who meet and do business with top executives and higher-income individuals. The object of this diversification is to be able to offer your clientele other resources for professional services, as well as to trade and share new clients with the other group members.

[S] *Product-oriented businesses.* You can also obtain leads from non-competing product-oriented (as opposed to service) and credit-oriented businesses that review their customers' financial statements in the interest of making a sale. Credit-oriented businesses such as these include auto-leasing brokers, auto dealers, equipment-leasing brokers, mortgage and loan brokers and bankers.

[S] *Leads clubs.* Many local communities have leads clubs that meet twice a month, typically early in the morning. These clubs consist of professionals like you who are interested in generating new business. The meetings are based on the philosophy that relationships should be cultivated with "centers of influence"—other professionals who have their own established client base, who serve their clients well and who have information to exchange.

14 GET INVOLVED WITH CHARITABLE OR CIVIC ORGANIZATIONS

Most of us want to get more involved in our communities, but we don't make the time. Consider, however, that you'll realize an indirect benefit from devoting some of your time to a civic or charitable organization. Not only will you be able to make a positive contribution to your community, but civic and charitable activities can also provide great opportunities for business contacts. Monthly chambers of commerce meetings, for example, provide a relaxed atmosphere in which you can meet potential clients and obtain referrals. Meetings of charitable organizations and other civic groups can also turn into worthwhile places for professional prospecting. You'll find that the common cause will contribute to building trust at a higher level between you and your prospect.

15   USE THE YELLOW PAGES

Some individuals have relied on the Yellow Pages alone as the exclusive means to develop prospecting lists. While certain people may feel that pursuing leads from the Yellow Pages isn't the most professional avenue to take, others have done so with great success. The Yellow Pages lists professional and product categories by area and provides a focused way of gathering information. For example, if you wanted to target your services to cosmetic surgeons in Nassau County, New York, you could use the Yellow Pages to assemble a list of all the cosmetic surgeons in the area and their addresses and telephone numbers.

[S] *Making yourself visible.* Help your prospects find you. Try to get a free listing in a business directory. Again, the Yellow Pages will provide valuable visibility. Competitors of the Yellow Pages, however, have recently begun to surface in many cities throughout the United States due to the increasing demand for more business resource directories. Many of them will provide you a free listing under your business category.

---

16 LOOK TO PROFESSIONAL ORGANIZATIONS AND CLUBS FOR LEADS

You may need to provide a free service to the organization or club of your choice in exchange for their list of members. The important thing is to get the list. For instance, suppose that you decided to target your services exclusively to people who make a hobby of intellectual pursuits. Try to obtain the list of MENSA members in your particular area in exchange for a free presentation to the local MENSA membership on a financial topic of interest. Or, as another example, suppose you targeted employees of the local telephone company; you might be able to obtain a list of their names from the credit union that exclusively serves them. Here is a strategy for obtaining such a list:

[S] *Start at the top.* Thomas P. Marth of The Mass Mutual in Las Vegas, Nevada, wanted to develop a list of prospects at a local workers' union. He had the clever idea to call on the union president and invite him out for coffee, explaining that he thought he could be of special service to the union members. Marth asked to review the provisions of the union's pension and medical insurance plans and then, using those points of reference, was able to implement a direct mail program, with the president's endorsement, to effectively address the financial service needs of the membership.

Another approach would be to become active in other financial advisers' professional organizations. Attending seminars, presentations and meetings held for professionals within your target market would provide you with the opportunity to meet some of the key players in organizations in which you have an interest. Arriving early would enable you to meet the speaker—who typically is among the first arrivals—gaining an introduction to a center of influence that might otherwise be hard to come by.

[S] *Joining an association.* Associations exist for almost every type of target group you can imagine. Covering business and trade, human services, professional resources, veterans and military organizations,

labor and political collectives, sporting groups and scores of other categories, associations can offer you a good way to approach members
of your target group. To find the local association that best fits your
target market, just look in the Yellow Pages under "associations."
You'll find many of them listed right there. To aid in your research, you
should also be able to find a copy of the *Directory of Associations* at
your local library.

17 INCLUDE YOUR CLIENTS' NEIGHBORS IN YOUR LIST OF LEADS

A financial planner we heard from in Honolulu, Hawaii, takes advantage of the large number of condominium residences in her area to build her list of leads and expand her client base. When she finds a new client who lives in a condo, she makes cold telephone calls to all the other residents in the building or complex. She obtains their phone numbers by using the *Cross-Reference Directory*, a directory published by the local phone company that provides names and telephone numbers listed by *address*.

The planner asks her existing client—or clients if she has more than one in the building—if that client would mind if she used his or her name. Then when she makes the cold calls, she tells her prospects that she has a client who's one of their neighbors who has been very pleased with the investment results she's obtained. This association proves to be a powerful door-opener. She lets her prospects know that she's calling for two reasons: first, to introduce herself and, second, to leave them with one good investment idea (typically for something that she knows will pique their interest, like a C.D. or Hawaii municipal bond). When she asks if they would like her to send additional information, they typically say yes.

18   Buy a List

List-selling direct mail companies abound, and their powerful computerized data bases allow mixing and matching a wide variety of specifi-
cations to create the exact type of list you need. R.L. Polk & Co., for
instance, a direct mail firm that has offices in 22 cities throughout the
United States and Canada, lists approximately 8.5 million businesses
and 70 million households in its data base. If you wanted to market to
tier III and IV prospects, you might consider buying a list of luxury car
owners in your area (even specifying a particular model and year if you
wanted). Lists of recreational vehicle, truck and motorcycle owners are
also available, as are lists for boat and airplane owners—all of whom
can make attractive prospects.

Lists are available for every product, service and professional category imaginable. Other examples of lists that you might get include
male or female heads of household (specified according to income
level, geographical location, residence type, type of car or number of
cars owned, number of children, etc.); senior citizens lists; and business lists for every type of business industry—including agriculture,
transportation, wholesale and retail trade, finance, insurance and real
estate, among many others.

Before you actually buy one, make sure that the list you're getting is
reasonably up-to-date. A good list-selling firm will typically guarantee
95 percent deliverability (i.e., you will receive a refund on the postage
you spend for any returns in excess of five percent).

TO GET STARTED...

1.   Identify your single best source of leads to date.

_____

2.   List the three best ideas in this chapter that you can use.

_____

_____

_____

3. List any additional ideas that occurred to you as you were reading the chapter.

   _____

   _____

   _____

4. Choose any two of the strategies listed above that you'd like to try. Identify the steps you'll need to take to implement them.

Strategy: _____

Implementation Steps:	Date To Complete:	Who Will Implement the Steps If Not You?
1. _____	1. _____	1. _____
2. _____	2. _____	2. _____
3. _____	3. _____	3. _____
4. _____	4. _____	4. _____

Strategy: _____

Implementation Steps:	Date To Complete:	Who Will Implement the Steps If Not You?
1. _____	1. _____	1. _____
2. _____	2. _____	2. _____
3. _____	3. _____	3. _____
4. _____	4. _____	4. _____

3 *Connecting with Your Market*

Members of your target market may not always behave the way you expect them to, or the way they're "supposed to," and for that reason you may need to spend time educating or "conditioning" them. The objective of conditioning a market is to establish boundaries and guidelines within which you can develop fruitful working relationships with your clientele. It will be up to you to set a tone for control, to let your clients know that they have to work with you and do what you expect in order for them to benefit from the association—for the association to be, in fact, mutually beneficial.

For instance, if you decide that you want to target a younger, baby-boomer-type of market, you may find that you'll have to spend substantial time educating the "carpe diem" (i.e., live for the day: literally, "seize the day") mentality out of these individuals and conditioning them to behave more providently. Younger investors are often far from conservative. They are often afflicted with the "yuppie syndrome," a malaise that causes its victims to believe they'll get rich overnight, influencing them to spend freely rather than save. Conversely, investors who are 55 years old and older tend to be excessively conservative about their finances. This could be due to several factors: They may feel they're nearing the end of their investment cycle; they may have come from the school of hard investment knocks; or perhaps they have learned from the mistakes they've seen others make.

We recently met a young computer salesman on a plane. His expensive suit, Rolex and self-assurance shouted success. When he discovered that we were in financial services, he began berating us, saying how all of the financial professionals he had met just wanted to make a quick sale and didn't know how to handle "valuable" clients like himself.

So we asked his income. He replied that he and his wife together made about $130,000 a year—a tidy sum, but it didn't seem to justify his behavior. We asked him how much they saved. He said, "Well to tell you the truth, we spend a lot."

We then asked how much he thought they *could* save yearly. He answered: "At least $40,000." We told him that a financial adviser helping him invest that amount at an average commission rate of say five percent, which would be high, would earn about $2,000 a year. But to be realistic, we added, it was more likely that he and his wife would only save at best $10,000, which would translate into a mere $500 income for the adviser—not an extraordinarily lucrative account. It was no wonder that the financial professionals he met just wanted to make product sales; given his attitude and behavior, they saw that it would be the only way they could deal with him. Furthermore, we asked if he were a financial professional, wouldn't he rather devote his time and energy to a more realistic and well-mannered retiring couple with combined savings of say $850,000 than to him and his wife who had nothing but bad spending habits and an attitude? (Okay, so we ganged up on him a little; but neither of us wears a Rolex.) On the other hand, we made it clear that if he wanted to embark on a long-term program and was willing to behave himself, he would be able to get a fine result and would be a good account for a financial adviser.

Because these younger markets often believe in instant success, they also tend to think that high risk only implies a high reward. You'll find that you'll need to impress upon them that high risk also implies just that—high risk. By educating the greed out of these younger target clients, you can often help them learn to make the investment decisions that are right for them. It could very well prove to be a challenge for you too because, as you know, a fine line exists between what sells and what the client really needs.

The real challenge lies in conditioning your young client or prospect to see how much consistent, safe investing will produce over time. You can accomplish this by using your computer or financial calculator to create a model of future financial security based on any reasonable assumptions the clients choose. Ask your clients to estimate how much they think they can save each year over a period of time. Suggest that they make one projection for their annual savings for the next five years, a second projection for the following five years, and a third projection for the five years beyond that and so on. Chances are, their projected yearly savings would increase over these incremental time periods. Using this information, you can then calculate their future net worths. For instance, you can show your clients that $12,000 invested each year ($1,000 per month) earning say 8 percent interest (with dividend reinvestment) will grow to $1 million in 26 years—or in 22.5 years if it earns 10 percent. You can point out that this type of consistent saving can position an individual at the prime of life with a substantial nest egg—even if the yearly savings rate doesn't increase, but remains at a constant $12,000 per year.

With older clients, you may have to educate out some of their conservatism. While many older people probably should maintain a conservative portfolio, it doesn't necessarily follow that every investment they make should be so conservative. For example, gold options are usually viewed as a risky investment, but a small holding in a substantial and otherwise conservative portfolio largely made up of fixed investment vehicles might just contribute some needed inflation protection.

19   HELP YOUR MARKET UNDERSTAND ITS INVESTMENT PSYCHE

It's important to spend time discussing your clients' investment history, objectives and fears. You'll have to make sure that your clients have a good understanding of risk-reward ratios and can determine where along the risk-reward continuum they feel most comfortable making investment decisions. Although it may seem elementary to you, you'll find it beneficial to explain to your more conservative clients that the price for minimal risk and safety of principal may be a correspondingly lower investment return. You'll need to communicate to them the fundamental axiom of investing: the greater the risk, the greater the reward; and, conversely, the lower the risk, the lower the reward.

Even with more aggressive investors, you'll need to reinforce these and similar principles. Investments are typically cyclical in nature; they go up and down, and the most important investment practice involves making decisions based on consistency, careful planning and emotional restraint. You'll find that in working with "high rollers," you may, from time to time, have to encourage your clients to behave like the aggressive growth investors they are. Everyone occasionally gets cold feet, and your clients should, on occasion, be reminded that risky investments never look risky when they've performed well. (California real estate often provides a prime example.) Conversely, if you work with conservative investors who are primarily concerned with safety of principal, you'll find that, from time to time when they see other people's investments performing better than their own, you'll have to remind them of the investment objectives and guidelines they've established for themselves.

Your clients' emotional temperaments are equally as important as their specific investment needs, and their investment decisions should reflect careful evaluation of these considerations. For instance, even though a particular client may, for reasons of high net worth or high income-earning potential, fall into the category of an aggressive growth, high-risk investor, he or she may have a low emotional tolerance for risk. Similarly, some clients may feel comfortable placing an investment and leaving it to their financial adviser's surveillance; others may need to receive daily updates on its performance. Here is one way to help your clients understand their investment psyches:

⬛ *Using the orange juice analogy to evaluate goals.* To illustrate the range of investment objectives and help clients identify and sort out their own investment priorities, you can use the Orange Juice Investment Rating Model (Figure 3-1). A conceptual model, it's designed to help you respond to the client who may expect everything from one investment, to illuminate and clarify the client's investment psychology, and to provide a basis for the client's understanding of differences between investments. In the model, the juice of an orange provides a graphic illustration of the range of possible investment objectives. It's a simple, but powerful tool that can allow an investor to compare the relative strengths of different investments according to the investments' ability to achieve certain goals.

The model simply and effectively compares a financial investment to an orange. No matter how it's sliced, an orange will produce only a given amount of juice—for our purposes, let's say that amount is six ounces. An investment, like an orange, will yield only a certain quantity of benefits. Within the six ounces of total investment "juice," there are three distinct types of benefits: (1) after-tax cash flow (i.e., dividends, interest or distributions that are sometimes tax-free or tax-deferred), (2) growth of principal and (3) safety of principal; you can think of them as three 4-ounce juice glasses. All investments provide these fundamental benefits, but different investments offer different proportions of each. How you achieve growth for your client, and at what level of risk, will depend on your client's own emotional and financial priorities. While any two investments may be promoted similarly, they may in fact have significantly different abilities to produce the advertised benefits.

The critical assumption the model makes is that all investments in the marketplace provide a finite amount of the three objectives (i.e., benefits): after-tax cash flow (over the life of the investment), capital growth potential and safety of principal, which are apportioned in different ways depending on the particular investment. The model does

Figure 3–1.   The Orange Juice Investment Rating Model

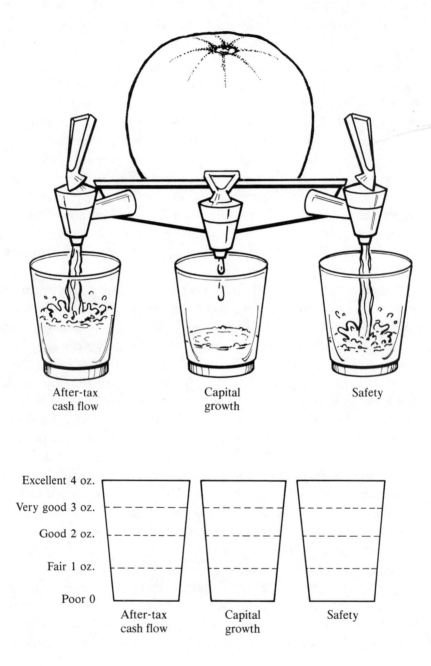

not allow for a "perfect" investment; it postulates that investors must always accept trade-offs in every investment. If you "squeeze" the orange in the direction of any one of these benefits, there won't be as much left over for the other two. In other words, if a certain investment offers a higher return in capital appreciation, it will necessarily offer fewer benefits in the areas of current cash flow or safety of principal.

Although this model discourages the natural tendency to believe we can pick an investment that's a "super winner," it's not an unrealistic model given that the actual performance of different investments over time tends to show more similarities than differences, and to bet that one can *always* pick the best investment is somewhat naive and can lead to poor portfolio diversification.

Additionally, the model only concerns itself with theoretical objectives. It does not predict actual results. The performance of any investment depends on the quality of the investment's management as well as on the occurrence of independent economic and fiscal events, which cannot be predicted at the time the investment is made. The model essentially serves a dual purpose:

- It enables an investor to clearly identify the types of investment objectives that are most important to him or her. This is something that few clients have ever done before. The model forces them to make trade-offs and come to terms with what's important to them.
- It gives the investor a way to evaluate the different benefits an investment that you select might produce, so that questions about management capability in light of future economic events can be examined in greater detail.

Once the model helps the client decide which type of investment to choose, it's still your job to help select the best vehicle to achieve the desired results.

Using the Model

Each investment is rated according to the three objectives: after-tax cash flow, capital growth and safety of principal.

You can allocate a total of six possible "ounces" (or points) among the three different objectives.

Each of the three objectives can receive up to four points (and half-points, where appropriate), according to the following scale:

4 = Excellent (within the top 20 percent of all investments that have the
        ability to yield that benefit)
3 = Very good
2 = Good
1 = Fair
0 = Poor (within the bottom 20 percent of all investments that have the
        ability to yield that benefit)

You should use a trial-and-error process to allocate the six ounces of investment juice among the three juice glasses (or benefits) until you achieve the most satisfactory trade-off of objectives for your client. Ask your clients to help make the benefit allocation until you're satisfied that it reflects their investment proclivity. With that accomplished, you can show them the different investments that fit their inclinations and address their needs.

In Figure 3–2, the model is used to compare a hypothetical municipal bond with a to-be-built real estate development, illustrating how easily you can conceptualize for your client the variances between different investments and investment objectives.

The investment objectives rating model is simple, yet it effectively forces an investor to take a close look at which investment objectives are most important and to review potential investments in terms of their trade-offs in relation to other investments. Our experience indicates that although investment markets are complex, the model enables clients to more thoroughly understand the benefits of given investment opportunities. Once clients have established their own personal rating system, they can begin to effectively evaluate the potential for particular investments to achieve their stated objectives.

With a little practice, you can become skillful at rating all investments that you incorporate into this model. Over time, your clients will begin to understand how the investments you recommend meet their needs. Incidentally, since no single investment may exactly match a client's ideal benefit profile, you can combine two or more investments cumulatively to produce the desired results.

Figure 3-2. Applying the Orange Juice Investment Rating Model

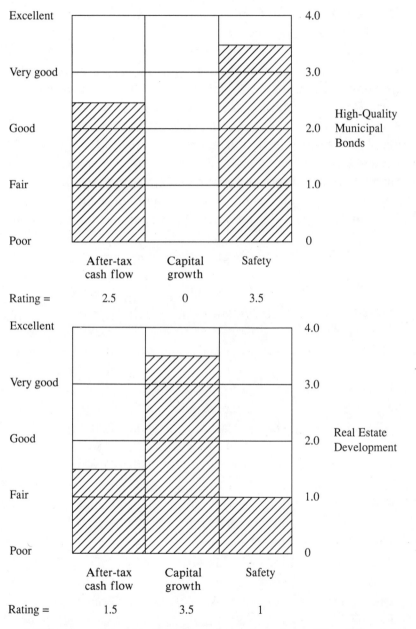

*Although municipal bonds could produce principal growth by virtue of changes in interest rates, one does not usually invest in municipal bonds with growth as an *objective*. For that reason, no allocation is made to this benefit category.

20 Talk to Your Clients in Language They Understand

All too often, financial professionals tend to get caught up in the jargon of the profession. It's easy to fall into the trap of using buzzwords that other financial professionals understand, but that may not make a lot of sense to clients. Show your clients that you're sensitive to their needs and have a vested interest in making sure they understand exactly what you're talking about. Conditioning them to trust you in this way will lay the foundation for good communication over the long term. A good way to begin, and a technique that often has the additional beneficial side effect of relieving some of the tension inherent in prelimi-

Figure 3–3.   The Investment Buzzword Generator

1. Adjusted	1. Depreciable	1. Accruals
2. Staged	2. Wraparound	2. Assets
3. Reportable	3. Crossover	3. Expenses
4. Sheltered	4. Managed	4. Risks
5. Tangible	5. Intangible	5. Write-offs
6. Leveraged	6. Recovery	6. Gains
7. Mortgaged	7. Underwriting	7. Notes
8. Allowable	8. Promissory	8. Liability
9. Deductible	9. Public	9. Costs
10. Legal	10. Deferred	10. Debt
11. Taxable	11. Development	11. Equity
12. Convertible	12. Capitalization	12. Capital
13. Improved	13. Acquisition	13. Losses
14. Leased	14. Unrealized	14. Proceeds
15. Registered	15. Liquidating	15. Dividends
16. Exempt	16. Preference	16. Cash flow
17. Discounted	17. Reinvestment	17. Bonds
18. Earned	18. Economic	18. Annuities
19. Passive	19. Portfolio	19. Distributions
20. Active	20. Private	20. Bonus

nary client meetings, is to use the Investment Buzzword Generator. This form (Figure 3–3) pokes fun at the use of buzzwords, which are not only misunderstood but frequently misused. The buzzword generator takes independently legitimate financial terms and combines them to create nonsensical phrases that often have an authentic "sound." It will demonstrate to your clients that not only do you have a good sense of humor, but—more importantly—you have a sincere interest in providing them with clear, understandable information.

The way to use the Investment Buzzword Generator is to ask your client to select three random numbers—each a number between 1 and 20. Then you match the number with the appropriate numbered term in the buzzword generator. For instance, the numbers 3, 8 and 15 would generate the phrase "reportable promissory dividends." Would your client consider these a desirable investment objective? How about the numbers 9, 16 and 1: "deductible preference accruals"?

The buzzword generator is also a good ice-breaker to use for a seminar or speech.

21   MAKE SURE YOUR CLIENTS LIKE YOUR RECOMMENDATIONS

As we previously mentioned, it's important to create a balance between what your clients want and what they need. Identifying what they like and listening to what they *want* will help you determine the level of their investment understanding and enable you to present investment recommendations that they will more readily accept. Clients often resist specific portfolio recommendations if they aren't familiar with the investment product or if they don't have a clear understanding of how it works.

The sample questionnaire that follows may give you some good ideas for questions that can help you key into your own clients' investment IQs. You would present each client with the questionnaire, asking him or her to fill it out.

Investment Familiarity Checklist

Please place a letter in the designated space next to each investment product listed below, as follows:

*   I —if, at any time, you've *invested* in it
*   A—if you haven't invested in it, but it *appeals* to you
*   U—if you're *unfamiliar* or *uncomfortable* with the investment (even if you've previously invested in it)

Please indicate one letter rating (I, A or U) for each investment listed.

_____   Annuities
_____   Antiques
_____   Art

Bonds:
_____   Corporate
_____   Municipal

_____   Coins (rare)

_____ Commodities
_____ Diamonds
_____ Foreign bank accounts
_____ Foreign securities (stocks or bonds)
_____ GNMAs ("Ginnie Maes," Government National Mortgage
     Association pass-through certificates)
_____ Gold (coins or bullion)

Mutual Funds:
_____ Income funds
_____ Balanced funds
_____ Growth funds

Oil and Gas:
_____ Income funds
_____ Oil and gas drilling partnerships

Real Estate:
_____ Real estate investment trusts
_____ Real estate limited partnerships
_____ Second mortgages
_____ Purchasing and managing your own properties

Other Partnerships:
_____ Cable TV
_____ Equipment leasing
_____ Venture capital
_____ Other

Savings:
_____ Passbook accounts
_____ Certificates of deposit
_____ Credit unions
_____ Managed securities accounts
_____ Silver
_____ Stamps
_____ Stocks
_____ Treasury bills
(continued)

Of all the investments you've made to date, which three have been the most beneficial for you?

1. _____
2. _____
3. _____

Why do you think so? _____
_____

Of all the investments you've made, which have been the least successful?

1. _____
2. _____
3. _____

Why do you think so? _____
_____

TO GET STARTED...

We believe the ideas in this chapter will go a long way toward helping you build a positive rapport with your clients. The Orange Juice Investment Rating Model, the Investment Buzzword Generator and the Investment Familiarity Checklist should all help you connect with and condition your market. To get started, adapt these forms to reflect your own particular circumstances and needs, and then test them on your clients and prospects. We're sure you'll be impressed with your results.

PART 2

External Marketing

4 *Seminars and Special Events*

At this point, we would like to make an important distinction between the two primary categories of promotional marketing: external marketing and internal marketing. External marketing describes the tools and techniques used to obtain new clients. Internal marketing does the opposite: building business by improving marketing and service to existing clients. Encompassing a variety of promotional strategies and materials, external marketing identifies and introduces your service to your non-referral prospects, creating a memorable image for it and eliminating the need to make cold calls.

In this chapter, we describe seminars and special events, both important components of an external marketing program. Chapters 5 and 6 continue the discussion of external marketing, focusing on a wide range and variety of additional marketing tools: the external media you create on your own (audiocassettes, videocassettes, brochures, newsletters and direct mail); and the external media that already exist for your use (advertising and public relations).

THE PURPOSE OF EXTERNAL MARKETING

External marketing is really about building credibility. In his audiocassette program entitled "The Great Salesperson," co-author Alan Parisse discusses his rules of selling. The first rule is to establish credibility because credibility lies at the heart of the entire sales and marketing process. The definition of credibility from Merriam-Webster's *Unabridged Dictionary* is "...the quality or power of inspiring belief; worthiness of belief." The synonyms for credibility tell even more. Can you think of a better basis for a long-term client relationship than the professional's being "believable," "honorable," "reliable," "well thought-of" and "trustworthy"? You want your clients and prospects to believe you. Credibility creates a condition that allows you to control the sales process; essentially, the more credible you are, the easier sales will be.

STICKING TO YOUR PLAN

Establishing a well-rounded external marketing plan will require a measure of self-discipline and commitment. You'll need to stick with your program when business is good and when business is bad. In tough times, it can be difficult to focus on marketing, and it may be harder still to find the necessary budget. In good times, it's easy to become complacent, especially when you're busy serving your clients. The important thing to remember is to pursue your marketing program regardless of how well you're doing—whether your goal is to initiate new business or to perpetuate the positive momentum you've already created.

SETTING A BUDGET

The budget you have to work with will determine the variety and quantity of marketing tools you can use, so first establish a ceiling for the *maximum* dollar amount you feel you can spend within a specified time frame—one year, for example. Then identify several materials that you'd like to test. Set a schedule for your program, itemizing the tools you're going to use during the year, their corresponding implementation dates and the response goals that you hope to achieve. Last, be sure to track your results to determine which of the tools selected worked best, and why. You should include in your tracking data the following types of information:

- Who responded positively (i.e., can you further narrow your target group to identify and classify those prospects who expressed an interest in your services?)
- The time of year, day of the week or even time of day when you obtained the best response
- The specific marketing tool that obtained the greatest response

This type of information will enable you to polish your external marketing efforts so that each time you reach out to a group of prospects you get an increasingly favorable return.

TARGETING FOR RESULTS

The bottom line in external marketing rests on precise market targeting; the more narrowly you define your market, the better your response rate is likely to be. For example, if you use the "shotgun" approach in direct mail, statistics show that your efforts on average will yield less than a one-percent response rate. If you use a well-planned, well-targeted approach and message, achieving a rate as high as ten percent isn't uncommon. When you're looking at a target group of 3,000, for example, this vast difference in percentages translates into 30 potential clients versus 300.

Repetition is a critical component of any marketing campaign. The first time a prospect hears your name or sees it in print (or meets you, for that matter), the experience may not make much of an impression. It's important, however, to remind that potential client of your existence and availability because everyone's circumstances continually change. And when the need for a financial professional arises, your name should be the one that first comes to the prospect's mind.

USING SEMINARS TO YOUR ADVANTAGE

As an external marketing tool, seminars are among the best ways to increase your credibility and position you as an expert within your community. For stockbrokers, seminars provide an especially valuable tool because people are often hungry for information about the stock market.

Consider sponsoring a seminar or workshop at least once or twice a year. Interestingly, many people don't like to attend seminars by themselves, so, with your encouragement, they'll bring a friend, relative or associate with them—increasing attendance and bringing in more prospects for you!

Obviously, finding a unique seminar topic and focusing on a subject that people really want to hear about will make a big difference. Make the event an *important* one, because doing something important will make people remember you.

The key to a good seminar is to motivate your audience. If you leave them wanting just a little bit more, you'll be enticing them to come in to your office.

22   GIVE AN EDUCATIONAL SEMINAR

As a means of establishing yourself as a knowledgeable community resource, your seminar can prove to be one of the most effective ways to promote the value of your professional services. Providing education tends to create substantial goodwill. The recipient of the educational experience remembers the sponsor positively and often wants to reciprocate.

Although no specific selling or promoting of financial services occurs at an educational seminar, the seminar itself is an effective advocate of intelligent financial services, and the attendees will often look to you to provide them with advice or consultation afterward.

[s] *Current economic topics.* Seminars on current financial problems can be very effective; present and explain the problem and then demonstrate how sound planning and investing can provide solutions. Here are some examples of possible topics:

- Why Social Security may not be available at retirement
- How to avoid getting hurt during another stock market crash similar to the one that occurred in October 1987
- The impact of a rising or falling dollar on investment opportunities
- The decline of defense spending: The impact of the peace dividend on investment dividends

Remember: Your topic should match your target market's interests or needs.

[s] *"How-to" workshops on money management.* These have a very broad appeal, drawing people from many different market segments. Subtopics covered could include easy tips for budgeting, goal-setting and saving, as well as investing in stocks, bonds and annuities.

[s] *Seminars on using software.* The variety of financial management computer software now available on the market also lends an opportunity for you to educate your clients and prospects. Sponsor a workshop

on how to use one of these software packages, establishing yourself as an educational resource for the workshop participants.

s *Sensationalist themes.* "Financial Preparedness for the Big Quake," "The Coming Stock Market Crash," "Financial Implications of the Electronics Revolution" and "Nuclear Waste: Potential Threat or Investment Opportunity?" are examples of unusual topics that could generate substantial interest and enthusiasm, setting you apart as a creative thinker. Sensationalist topics would typically warrant the combined efforts of several professionals offering different, complementary areas of expertise; for the topics listed above, for example, professionals in the fields of finance, geology, physics and electronics would make valuable combined contributions.

Try to prepare for the next big economic event. For example, if the stock market crashes again, or a major oil shock occurs, could you put together a timely seminar within a week? Anticipate such an event by making an outline of the topics and subtopics that would be of interest to your market, lining up your professional resources so that they can contribute to your efforts too. If the event comes to pass, you'll get a lot of recognition for being among the first to analyze its impact and educate your community, and you'll draw a large audience!

s *Health care insurance.* A seminar on long-term health care and disability insurance should attract the retired or soon-to-be-retired market, as well as middle-income families who have concerns about aging relatives.

s *Pre-retirement.* Easily targeted to corporations, unions and other public groups, pre-retirement seminars should be presented by a team of professionals, all selected by you and all supportive of your pre-retirement planning philosophy. The team could consist of a physician, a lawyer and a representative of the Social Security Administration; each would provide invaluable information on preparing for retirement. You would be the seminar leader and facilitator, bringing it all together. Many corporations would be interested in this type of professionally planned educational program.

s *Post-retirement.* Perhaps a local chapter of the American Association of Retired Persons might even sponsor the seminar for you, underwriting some of its expenses (such as those associated with location, promotion and refreshments). Or try speaking at a retirement community. Information presented could range from investments to insurance to estate and tax planning.

s *Planning for college.* Seminars on preparing for college expenses will appeal to people with children nearing college age. You can expand this market even further by inviting people who have just recently become parents or who have children in day-care. One way to cultivate a list of new parents is to contact directors of local day-care centers and offer to conduct seminars for the parents.

Robert C. Monin, a financial planner in Williamsville, New York, buys time on the local cable TV station to present a 30-minute seminar on repositioning assets in order to qualify for increased amounts of college financial aid. His own firm's broadcast has resulted in many new clients, and the videocassette is also being used by the local high school during the school's "parents' night."

Alternatively, you can tailor your presentation to appeal to a narrower market segment—to parents, for example, who plan to have their children attend Ivy League or other private colleges (which have high capital requirements), or to parents of children who have physical disabilities and special educational needs. Depending on your focus, this type of seminar can draw any number of different target groups.

s *Financial services for the newly widowed.* Try presenting generic financial services seminars for groups of widows and widowers. Often, after a spouse has passed away, the remaining spouse has a great need for sensitive and caring financial advice. The same holds true for the newly divorced; there often exists a significant need for financial assessment and planning.

s *Retirement planning for temporary office workers.* Contact employment agency owners or managers and offer to present a free seminar to the agency's temporary workers on how they can set up their own retirement plans independently of the companies they work for.

⬚ *Corporate workshops.* One financial planner mails out 25 letters every week to local businesses and associations informing them of his availability to speak, free of charge, at workshops or seminars for their employees or members. He promotes the fact that he doesn't sell any products in the workshop.

For corporations, you can volunteer to promote the employer's benefit package as part of your presentation.

You can also emphasize your offer to be a "fill-in" for any speaker who cancels at the last minute. Every organization gets faced with last-minute crises in which you can become a hero. If you don't hear from these organizations within three months of your initial contact, do another mailing to them. Persistence pays.

⬚ *New business owners.* Present a seminar for new small business owners. This would be particularly effective if presented in tandem with an attorney and CPA. Information presented might include these topics:

- Tax aspects of the different forms of business ownership and compliance with the Internal Revenue Code
- Employee benefit programs
- Personal benefits payable with business dollars
- Maximizing retirement plan benefits
- Reasonable compensation issues and employers' responsibilities
- Cash-flow problems
- Tax-planning ideas

⬚ *Tax-advantaged investments.* Offer a seminar on the strengths and weaknesses of the various types of tax-advantaged investments still available, illustrating how investment suitability depends on the investor's risk tolerance level.

⬚ *Savings and retirement planning for the self-employed.* This type of workshop has a very broad market appeal. For one specific approach, you could request five to ten minutes at weekly meetings of local real estate salespeople to talk about the benefits and options of tax-deferred savings, which they can take advantage of as self-employed individuals. You might even show a group such as this a way to invest their retirement funds in a real estate program.

⬛ *Investment options for corporate pension and profit-sharing plans.* This offers a great opportunity for involvement in asset management. You can tailor your presentation to meet the specific needs of just one corporation you're prospecting to, presenting your information to policymakers within that organization. Alternatively, you can create a generic seminar that targets a broader-based audience, which might consist of all small- to mid-sized organizations with employee benefit plans, or organizations that want to establish employee benefit plans, in your market area.

⬛ *Financial management for your clients' children.* Developing a planning, investment or money management seminar for college-age children will provide them with a valuable service. Moreover, these children will soon become active contributors to the economy within their chosen professions and could very well become future clients. Not only can your seminar help make their transition easier from a protected financial environment into a world of independence and autonomy, but when they eventually require professional financial expertise you'll be the first person they call. Encourage the parents, as well as the children, to attend.

23   INVITE A GUEST SPEAKER

A way of boosting attendance, having a guest speaker can also enhance your reputation as a professional who's eager to serve the community. You may want to hire an expert to speak on a topic that's
relevant to the seminar material. An economist, for instance, may
boost attendance. Or you could invite a physician specializing in geri-
atrics to speak at a retirement seminar. Remember too that celebrity
sells. Featuring a speaker with a recognized name always encourages
attendance.

When Pat Qualls became an independent financial planner in Car-
mel, California, she recognized the value of sponsoring a major event
with a well-known speaker as an investment in her own success.
Staunchly believing that clients are the most important asset of a business, she wanted to make her own clientele feel very special. Her goal
was to provide them with the best information that would allow them
to make intelligent and informed investment decisions—ultimately
making her job easier as well.

Qualls' major event was a seminar/dinner to commemorate the
birthday of Adam Smith, the 18th-century philosopher often thought
of as the father of modern economics. Following her intuition that
style communicates everything, she made sure that the invitations re-
flected the tenor of the event. They featured a picture of Adam Smith
on embossed, gold foil-stamped paper and invited clients and their
guests to come hear Bob Neurock from "Wall Street Week." The envelopes were all hand-addressed and hand-stamped. This attention to
style paid off royally because she received a 20-percent to 25-percent
response.

The concept was so unusual that the local press covered the event,
and people talked about it for weeks afterward. Qualls had spent a
great deal of time and money, but this investment in her own image as
a financial professional paid for itself many times over in new clients.

A strong advocate of community education in general, she continued to sponsor regular educational seminars and workshops. She
would solicit input from her own clients to assess their educational

needs and then sponsor relevant workshops for the community at large. Continuing to offer educational opportunities proved her conviction that the more Pat Qualls gave to her community, the more people would want to give to her. It was a strategy that worked phenomenally well.

[s] *Moderating a debate.* Although it's usually prudent to make certain that a guest speaker's views are consistent with yours, you might consider trying a different, more unusual tack. You could invite two experts with widely differing views to debate a particular issue that you would moderate. The divergence of views would underscore the need for a financial professional to help investors sift through the complexities and quantities of information, as well as to help them through times of economic uncertainty.

Sponsoring any guest speaker will typically cost you some money, but it will increase audience draw and enhance your reputation in ways that will make the cost insignificant. To reduce the initial cost, however, you can always sponsor the seminar in conjunction with one or several other financial professionals and share the leads generated from the event.

---

24   PRESENT THE SEMINAR AS A JOINT VENTURE

Not only will this defray some of the costs associated with presenting the seminar, it can also strengthen your image and simply increase attendance. For instance, presenting the seminar in concert with an accounting or law firm would demonstrate your professionalism as well as your access to other skilled resources. This type of seminar venture allows you to focus on technical subjects using the support and expertise of other professionals.

[S] *Accounting firms.* During the months of September or October, as the calendar year draws to a close, you might present a seminar that would describe year-end tax and investment strategies to maximize tax benefits. The seminar could feature several presentations—by an accountant, an attorney and a financial planner—and would have a broad-based market appeal. You could sponsor the seminar with an individual accountant or with an accounting firm. If you joint-ventured the event with a major accounting firm, you might be able to get the firm to pick up the larger share of the costs. An accounting firm would also help increase attendance by promoting the event to its own clientele.

[S] *Small banks.* Many small, newly formed banks, private banks and private banking divisions of larger financial institutions aggressively promote their services to obtain sophisticated clients. You might be able to develop a relationship with such a bank to sponsor a series of breakfast or luncheon seminars educating consumers on a variety of financial topics.

[S] *Unrelated business concerns.* Alternatively, you may decide that a more novel approach would be to sponsor a seminar with an unrelated business entity, creating an unusual, memorable seminar combination. "Fashion and Finance," for example, could combine a financial seminar with a fashion show; the clothing designer or retailer might underwrite the costs of the seminar, which could be held at a country club, and you would guarantee the presence of an audience. Another possible seminar combination would be "Art and Investments." Held at an art gallery that featured a special exhibit, the seminar could focus on the different facets of charitable giving of artwork.

s *Charitable organizations.* Try to get a charitable organization to cosponsor the seminar; the organization would promote the event and collect the profit from the admission proceeds, net of expenses. You would benefit from the seminar exposure, without incurring any out-of-pocket cost, and you would also have the opportunity to follow up with the seminar attendees later. Another advantage to such cosponsorship is that the implied endorsement of your services by the charitable organization may increase your credibility.

---

25   SPECIALIZE AND TARGET FOR THE GROUP YOU WANT TO DRAW

The seminar can be one targeted expressly for a particular market. Examples include dentists, presidents of corporations, corporate executives or members of a retirement community. Be specific, and let the recipients of the seminar invitation know that the seminar is exclusively for them.

The list of potential seminar targets is long, but might include:

- The newly divorced
- The newly widowed
- The to-be-married (for structuring prenuptial agreements or tax and estate planning)
- Parents of college-bound children
- Individuals wishing to establish living trusts
- Owners of small- to mid-sized businesses with employee benefit plans
- Owners of small to mid-sized businesses who wish to develop benefit plans
- Medical, business or engineering students (for money management or business planning)
- Pet owners who wish to provide for their animals in the event of their death or disability

Beyond properly targeting your audience, you'll need to key your presentation specifically to that audience, to identify the needs of the audience. As a means to accomplish this, you can include with the seminar invitation a request for the invitee's participation. For instance, the invitation might say, "If you submit a question on the enclosed return form with your registration, I guarantee that I'll address it during the seminar." At this time, you should also include a preliminary survey form to obtain information about the seminar registrants. Each audience is different; surveying your audience before your presentation will enable you to better address the group's specific needs and to increase attendance.

⟦s⟧ *Surveying the group.* Create a questionnaire to discover what seminar topics have the greatest interest and appeal for your target group. You can list approximately ten topics in the questionnaire and ask respondents to check off three. Have your list printed in two different ways; in the second version, the order of possible seminar topics would be the reverse of the order in the first version of the form. This will guard against the natural tendency that people have to check off the first items they see, and should provide you with a more objective response. The advantages to using this type of questionnaire are that it will enable you to focus your seminar topic on what your target really wants to hear, and it will serve as a "drip" on your prospects (see Strategy 40).

⟦s⟧ *Seminars in translation.* James Burke, a CFP and attorney in Campbell, California, offers the following idea for a way to reach markets that are often hard to crack. You can offer seminars on any number of financially meaningful topics to members of the general public (perhaps within your target group) who are hearing-impaired. The seminar would be designed specially for them. Your presentation would be electronically amplified; as you spoke to the group and presented your information using slides, overheads, videos—or any other combination of techniques you chose—the attendees would listen through individual headsets, which you supplied to them when they arrived, enabling them to adjust the volume to a level appropriate for them.

By the same token, you could create a seminar like this for members of a non-English-speaking community in your area. For this type of seminar, you would need a translator who would translate your English words into language the seminar attendees understood. Again, you would use a special amplification system—but in this case it would be for the translator.

You might also choose to present a seminar using sign language, if your target audience has that need.

⟦s⟧ *Corporate questionnaires.* As a professional speaker, co-author Alan Parisse offers a repertoire of several presentation topics that lend themselves to different adaptations in tone and content. In preparing to speak to corporate groups, he sends a preliminary questionnaire to the company's policymakers. The response to this questionnaire—which requests information ranging from average age, experience and income level of the seminar attendees to their taste in humor—guides the manner in which Parisse tailors his presentation. It additionally demonstrates his ability and willingness to deliver a presentation that will meet the specific goals and expectations of the company. A shortened version of his questionnaire is shown in Figure 4–1.

Figure 4–1.   Speaker's Information Survey

[Your Name and Address Here]

■   **SPEAKER'S INFORMATION SURVEY**   ■

[Name of Firm or Organization]

Please help me to do my best at your meeting by doing the following:

1. Put me on the mailing list to receive all pertinent information regarding the event or program.
2. Send me any internal publications that you feel may be of help in personalizing my presentation.
3. Complete the enclosed questionnaire as fully as reasonably possible. Please feel free to give approximate answers and to skip any questions that do not apply or that would require you to divulge confidential information.
4. Call or write with any additional information.

Thank You,

[Your Name]

Figure 4-1.   Speaker's Information Survey (Continued) ·

QUESTIONNAIRE

■   THE PRELIMINARIES

Name of firm _____

Contact person(s) _____

Telephone: Office __(___)_____ Night before meeting __(___)_____
                                    (FOR EMERGENCY USE ONLY)

The meeting starts on _____ _____ _____ _____ at _____
                         Day   Month   Date   Year   Time

My speech starts on   _____ _____ _____ _____ at _____
                         Day   Month   Date   Year   Time

Location of meeting _____

Distance and time from the airport (approx.) _____

Who will be introducing me? _____

Who is the person responsible for room set-up and logistics? _____

Do they have my *Ideal Stage Set-Up* flier? _____
(if not, please give them the attached copy)

Does he or she have my suggested introduction?   ☐Yes   ☐No
(if not, please give them the one attached)

Please send us a detailed program. If a detailed program is *not* available, please complete this section. Concerning the other speakers' backgrounds, state if they are internal or outside speakers, and if they are representing a product.

Speaker *before* me	Topic	Background
Speaker *after* me	Topic	Background
Other keynote	Topic	Background
Other major speaker	Topic	Background

Is this a periodic meeting (i.e., annual, monthly, etc.)? If so:

Who was the speaker in my slot last month or year? _____

What did he or she speak about? _____

How well was that speaker received? _____

To what do you attribute their level of success? _____

Figure 4–1.   Speaker's Information Survey (Continued)

QUESTIONNAIRE

■   DESCRIBE YOUR FIRM OR ORGANIZATION

In lieu of, or in addition to completing this section, please send me any promotional brochures or product offering literature that would give me the background I need on your organization and its product or service.

(If your organization is a subsidiary of a larger organization, please report on the subsidiary. If there is something about the parent organization that you feel is important for me to know, please list it separately.)

1. Years in existence _____

2. Primary business or purpose _____

3. Number of employees _____

4. If a trade or service organization, number of members _____

5. Please describe the type of people in the audience (i.e., professions, interests, level of financial sophistication) _____

_____

_____

6. Humor Style
    Good taste is always an objective and so is good humor. The problem is that the boundaries of good taste and politeness vary from group to group and from time to time. Please rate your group's humor style on a scale of one to ten, with one being truck drivers at a truck stop and ten being a church social. _____
    (1–10 Rating)

    Comments: _____

    _____

    _____

7. Please note anything else you feel I should know about the audience. _____

_____

_____

_____

Courtesy of Alan J. Parisse.

26   GIVE A PRODUCT SALES SEMINAR

This type of seminar is designed primarily to promote a particular product. Make sure the product is exceptional and well-targeted to the audience (e.g., present a marina limited-partnership offering to boat owners or promote a genetic engineering research and development venture to biochemists).

Or consider sponsoring a "product-mix" seminar by inviting a few product wholesalers who will give 10-minute to 20-minute highlight presentations so that the seminar attendees get a flavor for current possible product solutions. The wholesalers might even be willing to contribute to the seminar cost.

STRATEGY

27 BE PERSISTENT IN YOUR EFFORTS TO INVITE SEMINAR ATTENDEES

You can optimize your seminar attendance by following these few simple procedures:

s *Following up.*

1. First, you should begin with a formal invitation that is well designed and effectively written to appeal to your target group.
2. When you receive a positive response, send out a letter of acknowledgment stating that the hotel (or wherever the seminar is to be held) has received the reservation; this communicates a subtle message of obligation to the attendee and deters "no-shows."
3. If you don't receive a response to your original invitation, send a follow-up letter saying something like, "We haven't heard from you and just wanted to remind you that the seminar on planning for your retirement (or whatever) is coming up in two weeks. Shall we expect you and a guest?" Be sure to enclose another RSVP card, but also give them the option to respond by telephone or fax.
4. Finally, the day *before* the seminar, have your assistant telephone the confirmed attendees to remind them of the next day's event.

s *Printing tickets.* To boost attendance, why not print tickets and send some of them out to select prospects and give others to your clients to pass along to their friends or business associates? Tickets often elevate the importance and uniqueness of an event. How many brokers or planners do you know who offer tickets for their seminars and workshops? Not many, we'll bet.

s *Prize drawings.* This could also encourage attendance. In order to maintain and promote the professional image you need to best serve your clients, the prize should be related to their financial needs. Here are some examples:

- A book on economics
- A year's subscription to a business periodical
- Tickets to a special business workshop or other suitable event
- A free one-hour consultation with a tax attorney, accountant, planner, broker or insurance specialist

28 HOLD THE SEMINAR IN AN UNUSUAL SETTING; OFFER IT DURING THE DAY

All too often seminars are held in hotels. Although hotels provide convenient locations and are well set up to host group events, they don't typically lend themselves to creating memorable impressions—unless of course the event is a particularly elaborate or unusual one (like the Pat Qualls seminar described in Strategy 23, for example).

⑤ *Offbeat locations.* For your seminar location, you could choose a place where people don't often go, but where they'd enjoy spending some time—a museum, a library having a special exhibit, a university or a country club. Banks are also impressive places to hold seminars.

⑤ *Seminar "weekend getaways."* Of course, you shouldn't completely write off the possibility of using a hotel. You might hold your seminar at a hotel at which you've negotiated a price discount so that seminar attendees can also spend the night as a short "weekend getaway." The idea is to be different; have your seminar in a location, and conduct it in a manner that sets you apart from everyone else, that makes the event a memorable one and that shows people how creative you can be.

Successful people tend to control their own schedules and are able to attend seminars, workshops and other events when they choose. For a mid-week seminar, presenting the event during the day may be a way for you to preselect your audience. You can also offer two sessions for the same seminar; one during the day, the other at night to appeal to the nine-to-five crowd who might constitute a significant portion of your target market. Experiment to see what works for your targets.

29   CHARGE ADMISSION

This is particularly effective for seminars presented as a series, as well
as for seminars promoted by the shotgun method. The cost can be as
low as $5 per person. Although charging admission might hurt atten-
dance a bit, it helps defray the cost of promoting the seminar, and,
even more importantly, it would ensure that the people who came were
really interested. Charging admission also contributes an additional
sense of value and credibility to the event.

Once each quarter, a broker we know in Milwaukee holds a series of
three-hour Saturday morning workshops that cover six basic investment topics. He charges $10 for each session, or $40 for all six, promoting the workshops by direct mail and in ads in the local newspaper.
The admission fee he charges offsets about two-thirds of his promotional costs.

STRATEGY

30   CREATE A POSITIVE, MEMORABLE IMPRESSION

The single greatest error most people make is trying to squeeze too much information into their presentation. Remember, a day later the seminar attendees will remember only a fraction of the specific information you gave them. What will stay with them for a long time is the way they felt about you and your overall presentation. Create a positive experience for them, and it will pay dividends for them and you.

S *Delivery.* It's important to make a good impression at the outset of your presentation. People will determine whether you're a good speaker or not by judging your delivery. After the first five minutes, you can relax, but those initial minutes are when the audience will be judging you.

S *Dress.* Be sure not to overdress or underdress. Generally, a good rule of thumb to follow is to dress so appropriately to the occasion that no one particularly notices or remembers your clothes, but only retains a positive impression of your professionalism.

S *Illustrating your message.* Stephen J. Hart, a planner in Hazen, North Dakota, gives Hershey's chocolate bars to attendees of his pre-retirement seminars. He then asks if they remember how much the same candy bar, perhaps a bit larger, cost when they were children. The answer is about five cents. It's a novel way to illustrate the need for good financial planning, and one that his prospects remember for a long time.

31   Use Humor Where Possible and Appropriate

Humor has a wonderful way of enlivening an audience that may be fading, and of punctuating points that you're trying to make. You'll find it easier to tell a good joke if you allow yourself to get comfortable with it. When you hear a joke that you like, *write it down*. Then practice telling it to your associates, friends and family; ask for their feedback and be sure to assimilate it. Typically it's best to use humor that specifically relates to the seminar topic, but occasionally even an unrelated joke will work well. Make sure, however, that you're sensitive to the humor appreciation level of your audience and that there is very little possibility that you'll cause offense.

Stories can provide a valuable way to illustrate examples and relieve both audience and speaker tension. One way to make it "safe" to tell a joke or story is to find one that so accurately makes an important point that even if the audience doesn't find it funny, they'll still appreciate the message. For example, Philip Hartwell, a financial planner in Torrance, California, always begins his presentations with an anecdote as a means to gain the audience's attention, goodwill, and to promote a frame of mind in which they are relaxed and open to receive information. Because many people aren't familiar with financial planning and want to know what it is, he often uses the following story to illustrate what sound financial planning can accomplish.

"Three fellows went on a moose hunt in Alaska," Hartwell begins. "A bush pilot took them out to a lake in a remote wilderness area and left them there for a week. At the end of the week, the pilot returned to find that each man had killed a moose. Somewhat surprised, the pilot said, 'Look, this is a small plane; it won't be able to carry such heavy cargo.' One of the hunters protested, 'But last year we had four moose, and the pilot agreed to carry us all.' So the bush pilot, not wanting to be outdone, agreed to load everything on board. He taxied around the lake two or three times to gain speed, opening the throttle wide to take off. The plane struggled heavily off the ground, barely cleared a cluster of trees and then crashed into a rock at the southern edge of the lake. As dust and broken rock settled around the plane, one of the moose hunters groaned, 'I can't believe it . . . The same thing happened last year.'

"The purpose of sound financial planning," ends Hartwell, "is to prevent you from making the same mistakes you did last year." This is so valid a message that even if the story fails to elicit laughter, it still makes a well-targeted point.

[S] *Our favorite stories.* The following three stories have served us well in our presentations over the years. We hope that you can get some mileage from them too.

1. **Describing how a financial professional can deal with price/cost objections**

    The competition typically pretends that it can deliver the same value at a lower price, and the truth is that they can't. They do lower their price, but they also lower their value to compensate for it. We like to give our audiences the example of the discount store owner who boasts, "We sell at cost." When quizzed about how he can do this and still make a profit, he explains, "We buy for less than cost."

2. **Illustrating that it's the basics that count**

    Vince Lombardi, one-time coach for the Green Bay Packers, called his team together during practice one day and, pointing to the ball, said, "Men, this is a football." One of the linemen interrupted, "Coach, can you go a little slower?"

    Obviously, this joke is best told to an audience of middle-aged football fans who know who Vince Lombardi was. But it can pointedly illustrate the need for sticking to the basics in an investment portfolio.

3. **Illustrating the axiom that "nothing gold can stay" and that all investments go up and down—often capriciously**

    There were two diamond brokers, Max and Sam, who met every day for lunch. One day, Max showed Sam a diamond ring that his wife had given him the day before for their 25th wedding anniversary. Sam examined it slowly and carefully, and when he was through, he offered Max $3,000 for it. Max said, "I'm sorry, but I can't sell it to you, Sam; it was a present from my wife."

The next day Sam greedily eyed the ring again and this time offered Max $4,000 for it. The offer was too good; Max couldn't resist, and he sold the ring.

About a week later, Max had begun to feel pangs of remorse that even his profit couldn't assuage. So he expressed his unhappiness to his friend.

"Look, Sam, I really need to buy that ring back from you. After all, it was a present from my wife."

Sam hesitated. "Well, I don't know. It's a pretty valuable ring, and I like it a lot."

"Sam, we're friends, right?" Max pressed. "I'll buy it back from you for $6,000."

It was a very good price, and Sam couldn't refuse, so he sold Sam back the ring. About two weeks later, Sam realized that he had made a mistake, that he should have held on to the ring longer, so he made Max a new offer—this time for $7,000. Max demurred for a while, but by the end of the lunch hour, he had sold it again to Sam.

Six months passed during which the two friends exchanged the anniversary ring maybe another half-dozen times. The price had gone up to about $20,000. And then one day Max tried to buy it back again.

"Sorry Max," Sam said, "I sold it."

"How could you sell it?" Max exclaimed in disbelief, "We were both making so much money off it!"

32   DON'T FORGET ABOUT SEMINAR ROOM SET-UP

This is as important as getting the clients to attend. The proper environment can have a dramatic effect on the attitude of the attendees and on your ability to communicate your ideas. Make sure the lighting is good; dull, underlit rooms prevent eye contact and inhibit your potential to shine. Make sure too that the temperature is about two degrees cooler than what feels comfortable; it's better to have people complain a little bit about the coldness of the room than to fall asleep.

Set chairs up for only 70 percent to 80 percent of the audience you expect (i.e., the confirmed attendees). Chairs for the other confirmed attendees should be stacked at the back of the room (or even better, in a back room) and only set out as people arrive and chairs are needed. It's difficult for a speaker to control a room with a lot of empty chairs in it. Creating a slight seating shortage forces people to sit closer to the front of the room, where you are, enabling you to make better eye contact with them. It's an insult to the speaker when the seminar attendees sit three or four rows back. Also, when latecomers arrive, it will be less disturbing to the people who are already there, since the late arrivals will be forced to sit in the back. Be aware too that 20 people in a room with 22 chairs looks like a success; 20 people in a room set up for 50 could look like a failure, no matter how good the seminar really is. Even if you have a turnout of 100 people, if the room contains too many extra chairs, it will look like you fell short of the mark.

Let the building management know what type of physical set-up you have in mind. Give them an illustration of how you would like to have the seminar room arranged to make it easy for them. An example is shown in Figure 4-2.

[s] *Outlines.* Hand out a simple, brief seminar outline with lots of space between the topic headings so that people can follow along and have something to refer to later on. Don't forget to include your name, address and telephone number on it.

An outline is useful because it provides the attendees with something tangible that they can take away with them, reducing their note-

Figure 4–2. Ideal Seminar Room Set-Up*

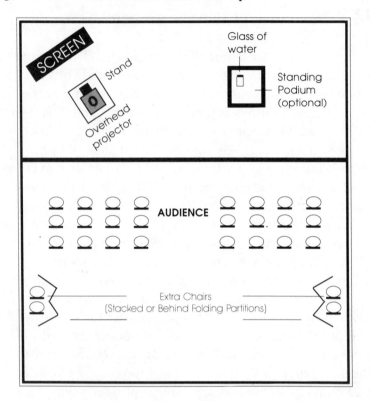

*The stage shown here is designed for a right-handed person; if you're left-handed, you should reverse the placement of everything on the stage. Obviously, this is only one way of setting up the stage, but it's something you can use for starters. Eventually, you'll probably want to modify the set-up to better accommodate your own individual style.

Courtesy of Richard Wollack and Alan J. Parisse.

taking obligation and allowing them to focus more on your presentation. If you know at the outset of your presentation, however, that you won't be able to cover all the points on your outline, tell your audience; it will lessen any potential disappointment.

Any additional information that you want to give the seminar attendees should be kept separate from the outline and handed out at the end of your presentation.

[s] *Visual aids.* Of all the visual aids available—easels, chalkboards, 35-millimeter slide projectors, videos and overhead projectors— overhead projectors will probably serve you best for most presentations. You can use an overhead projector without dimming the lights, thus enabling you to maintain eye contact with your audience. It also allows you to continue facing your audience, rather than turning your back as you would, for instance, with an easel or chalkboard, and to control where the audience is looking. Be sure, however, to turn off the projector when you don't specifically need it, in between points that require illustration, for example, since leaving the projector on while you're talking can be a distraction.

It's easy and inexpensive to make your own overhead transparencies. Once you have the original artwork or text, you can create transparencies using a photocopying machine and special overhead transparency film. Art supply stores typically carry boxes of transparency film for plain paper copiers, available in quantities of approximately 100 sheets per box.

For very large audiences of 250 or more, an overhead projector may not provide a clear enough image unless the hotel can provide an extra-large screen; in this case you may find that using a slide projector is more appropriate. Most importantly, keep the slides or overhead transparencies very simple (the fewer words, the better).

[s] *Guest books.* This will give you a record of who attended and enable you to follow up by contacting them later on. Also, have a stack of appointment request cards available and in plain sight for all the seminar attendees.

[s] *Seminar souvenirs.* It's important to give your audience something that will remind them of you later, something that will keep your name and telephone number within easy reach. Promotional giveaways like notepads, notebooks or binders work well. Hand these out to the seminar attendees and have an extra supply available at the back of the room as well. One San Francisco broker we heard about spends quite a bit extra to give attendees a Leatherette notepad holder imprinted with his firm's name and logo. He finds that his prospects value and keep this giveaway.

33   CONVERT THE SEMINAR ATTENDEES INTO CLIENTS WITH HOMEWORK

The homework should be in the form of a questionnaire or data form to be filled out by the seminar attendees in order to gauge their financial health, past and present, with an indication of future goals. This exercise will help personalize what they learned during the seminar, bringing a lot of information into sharper focus; it will also bring them, as prospects, closer to an appointment with you. This strategy works especially well for seminars that are held over two or more days.

34   ASK FOR AUDIENCE EVALUATION

Solicit feedback from your audience on the seminar presentation. You can obtain feedback most effectively by using an evaluation form that seminar participants fill out toward the end of your presentation. You can take out five or ten minutes before you make your concluding remarks to have them complete the form; this ensures that they'll do it before they leave. The questions might include the following:

1. How successful was the seminar at meeting your needs?
   ☐ Excellent
   ☐ Good
   ☐ Fair
   ☐ Poor

2. How did it rate in meeting your expectations?
   ☐ Excellent
   ☐ Good
   ☐ Fair
   ☐ Poor

3. What was the most valuable thing you learned? _____
   _____

4. How would you rate delivery of the information, including the use of visual aids and humor?
   ☐ Excellent
   ☐ Good
   ☐ Fair
   ☐ Poor

5. How would you rate the comfort of the seminar room?
   ☐ Excellent
   ☐ Good
   ☐ Fair
   ☐ Poor

6. Was the location convenient? Yes ☐ No ☐
   Comments: _____
   _____

7. What would you suggest to improve the presentation? _____

_____

_____

8. Would you be interested in seminars on other financial topics and products (listing what they are)? _____

_____

9. Would you like to be kept on a mailing list for future seminar invitations, newsletters, financial service news, etc.?
   Yes ☐   No ☐

10. Would any of your friends, relatives or business associates appreciate being placed on the mailing list?   Yes ☐   No ☐

_____

_____

11. Do you need any assistance in financial matters?
    Yes ☐   No ☐   Not sure ☐

12. Any other comments? (We can only improve our seminars through your feedback. So if you have any comments—positive or negative—please don't hesitate to share them with us.)_____

_____

_____

Using a questionnaire like this provides invaluable information. It will enable you to evaluate the success of the seminar and will provide you with the names of interested prospects. Also, it gives you the key interests of each attendee to store in your data base or files, and to help you plan future seminars. For example, when you accumulate enough questionnaires that indicate an interest in a certain investment topic, you would be able to offer the seminar and know that you'd have a ready-made audience for it.

35   IF YOU DON'T FEEL COMFORTABLE CREATING YOUR OWN SEMINAR, GET A PACKAGED ONE

Several firms commercially produce seminar packages that offer you step-by-step assistance in all aspects of seminar production. Using a prepackaged seminar is a good way to break into the seminar circuit and quickly develop a professional presentation. Financial Information Group, for instance, in Berkeley, California, sells four different seminar kits, covering retirement planning, real estate, fixed-income investing and college funding. The basic kit for each includes presentation graphics, seminar attendee workbooks, tips for marketing and presenting the seminar, sample ads, prospect letters and telephone scripts. Additional materials, including overhead transparencies or 35-millimeter slides, are also available for an extra fee.

Successful Money Management Seminars of Portland, Oregon, offers more deluxe seminar packages. One of the seminar packages is a broad-based program on financial planning and investment options. Also offered are seminars for business owners, asset preservation and retirement planning strategies. The seminar packages include the following:

- Operations and marketing manuals
- A speaker's manual
- Seminar script and notes
- Overhead transparencies that correspond to the script
- Attendee workbooks and homework packets
- Audiocassettes and videocassettes of the seminar (to be used for practice)
- Advertising and promotional materials

Quite a few financial planners have obtained positive business results from presenting these seminars.

Other firms that offer prepackaged seminars include Dearborn Financial Publishing in Chicago, Illinois; and Emerald Publications in San Marcos, California, which offers an entire series of seminar packages. Many of these firms limit the number of seminars that can be used in a particular area, protecting against oversaturation by local competition.

Aubrey Morrow, a certified financial planner and president of Financial Designs of San Diego, California, a full-service financial advisory firm, has had tremendous success in using this type of ready-made seminar and gets as many new leads as he can handle from them. Using Emerald Publications seminars, Morrow's presentations focus on living trusts, estate planning and money management. Presented with a living trust attorney, the seminars are given as a series consisting of seven workshops per week—two each on Tuesdays, Wednesdays and Thursdays (in the afternoon and evening) and one on Saturday morning. Sharing the costs with the participating attorney, Morrow uses an in-depth advertising campaign to promote the seminars, making use of radio, television and local newspaper ads, as well as direct mail invitations. Each seminar draws approximately 100 attendees who, at the conclusion of the seminar, are asked to fill out an evaluation form and indicate if they would like to receive a complimentary one-hour consultation with a certified financial planner. Approximately 60 percent indicate they do, and of that number the vast majority become Financial Designs' clients.

Other services will help you promote your seminar by providing you with invitations, a mailing list, business-reply cards, and hand-stamped outgoing envelopes, handling all components of the mailing for you. Seminars Plus in New City, New York, is one such service.

Although enlisting the help of a promotional and direct mail service can be helpful, freeing up your valuable time for additional marketing or client fulfillment, we like to encourage financial professionals to create and develop their own seminar presentation rather than buying a prepackaged one. As good as some of these prepackaged products may be, there is often no substitute for personalization and your own unique touch. Further, creating a seminar based on a current economic event or involving a particularly special concept will make the seminar more appealing to your target market.

STRATEGY

36 Offer Your Services as an Adult Educator

Continuing education is big business. A lot of adults look to credit-granting institutions for education in financial products and services. Instructors benefit by long-term exposure to serious, tuition-paying students, who also often happen to make good prospects. Call your local university or community college to let them know that you're well qualified and prepared to deliver a high-quality educational service to their students. You may even get paid for it. Remember, however, that your job will be to produce the educational results the institution and the students expect. You won't need to do more than let your students know what you do for a living. Numerous financial professionals who recommend this idea claim that if you do your teaching job well and earn their respect, your students will seek you out for a professional relationship.

s *Getting into the lecture circuit.* Many local organizations might be interested in having you as a guest speaker. These could include religious, civic or educational groups. Contact the organization's program planner and ask about upcoming events; request consideration as a speaker and then send out a media kit. If you're accepted, you can then help the organization publicize the event.

Many corporations seek the expertise of financial professionals to provide employee seminars or workshops on a variety of financial topics. You can send letters of inquiry to speaker bureaus or directly to key corporate policymakers to offer your speaking services. A clever way of distinguishing yourself is to include an audiocassette recording of one of your past presentations and a written outline indicating what you have in mind for that particular organization. Alternatively, you might provide brief synopses of three or four possible topics to increase the odds that they like one of your ideas. Including such items will show that you're serious, thoughtful and thorough, and it will give the recipient a foundation on which to judge your abilities.

You should mold your presentation to address the different needs of different organizations so that you speak to issues that are of particular concern to them. A Speaker's Information Survey, like the one shown in Figure 4-1, can help you do this. Make it easy for the organization to host your presentation. Let the staff member facilitating the event know how you would like the room and stage arranged. For this purpose, you can provide an illustration of your ideal room set-up (like the one shown in Figure 4-2). In addition, offer the facilitator a pre-written introduction, again to simplify the process for that person—as well as to ensure that the facilitator has something to say about your background and can pronounce your name correctly!

Jason H. Kurchner, a CFP in Saratoga Springs, New York, hires a public relations firm to set up speaking engagements for him. The firm handles all the details of the process, from making initial contact to arranging the actual speaking dates and times. He finds this arrangement the most productive in terms of the number of speaking engagements obtained. This higher productivity results for two reasons. First, a good P.R. firm has many well-established contacts. Second, a third party can often promote you better than you can promote yourself.

37 CREATE A SPECIAL EVENT

Periodically sponsoring a special event can generate a great deal of excitement about your practice. Although certain events will require you to make a substantial financial investment, people will remember them and, most notably, will remember *you* as being different from other practitioners in your field.

S *Picnics and barbecues.* Johannes Fure of Fure Financial Corporation in Eden Prairie, Minnesota, sponsors a local weekend "payday" picnic with live music. He advertises the event with fliers sent out to local businesses and charges approximately $4 per person. At the picnic, Fure hands out material that he has available concerning financial resources in general and his services in particular, and he makes sure that he and all of his associates and employees wear identifying name tags, just as they would at a seminar.

Robert B. Anderson of Capital Planning Group in Paradise, California, suggests hosting a special barbecue exclusively for clients and their guests. He sends each client an invitation with four tickets apiece, urging them to invite guests. In Anderson's experience, most of them bring friends—additional prospects for him.

Consider inviting product wholesalers to your picnic or barbecue. You may even be able to ask them to contribute to the picnic cost, but you should keep the event informal and require that they don't set up booths. The next time you host a product sales seminar, your clients may very well feel more comfortable and trusting of the wholesalers.

S *Parties.* Every year, Doug Hesse of Hesse Financial Advisors in Roswell, Georgia, organizes a "client appreciation" dinner. In 1989, he rented a paddle-wheel showboat on Stone Mountain Lake in Atlanta and hired a piano player and singer for entertainment. Approximately 150 clients attended. Hesse also invited five product sponsors to the event; each contributed $600 to help defray the costs of the evening, and each also contributed a small prize for a drawing that was held during the evening. In order to qualify for the drawing, the guests had to put the name of one referral, with their own, in the lottery. The major prize was a $1,000 zero coupon bond presented by Hesse Financial Advisors. Hesse has found that sponsoring this type of event solidifies his relationships with his best clients and also provides him with numerous qualified referrals (in 1989, he received more than 80).

⑤ *Free drawings.* Another financial planner, Frank D. Olesuk in Crystal Lake, Illinois, attends trade shows and expos where he gives out investment literature and sponsors free drawings for $100 worth of mutual fund shares. The drawing has provided him with free radio and newspaper publicity, and he estimates that as a result 75,000 to 100,000 people hear about his business each year.

⑤ *Blood drives.* If you share a building with other corporate tenants, you can sponsor a voluntary blood donor campaign to be held in your offices. The blood drive organization will provide refreshments, and you will benefit by having a captive audience of donors. Charles Scarborough of IDS Financial Services in Austin, Texas, claims to have used this method successfully. Other charitable events that you can sponsor that might get you some good community recognition and P.R. include fund-raising raffles for charitable organizations or food or clothing drives.

⑤ *High school essay contests or "economics fairs."* Competing students between the grades of nine and 12 could write and submit essays on a topic of current economic interest. You, or an individual of your choosing, would judge the entries, awarding first, second and third prizes. The event would garner some valuable local publicity. You might even get a local radio station to sponsor an on-the-air reading of the first-prize entry by the winning student.

You could also help organize a high school economics fair, either in connection with the essay contest, or as an independent event. Like a science fair, an economics fair promotes economic awareness among the students and their parents. The community exposure is extraordinary.

TO GET STARTED...

1. If you've had experience presenting seminars or special events, which has been your most successful one to date? _____

    _____

2. List several topics for your next few seminars. _____

    _____

3. Identify three (or more) key ways to boost attendance.

    _____

    _____

    _____

4. List the three best strategies in this chapter that you can use.

    _____

    _____

    _____

5. List any additional strategies that occurred to you as you were reading the chapter. _____

    _____

6. Choose any two of the strategies from the list you made for #5 that you'd like to try. Identify the steps you'll need to take to implement them.

Strategy: _____

Implementation Steps:	Date To Complete:	Who Will Implement the Steps If Not You?
1. _____	1. _____	1._____
2. _____	2. _____	2._____
3. _____	3. _____	3._____
4. _____	4. _____	4._____

Strategy: _____

Implementation Steps:	Date To Complete:	Who Will Implement the Steps If Not You?
1. _____	1. _____	1._____
2. _____	2. _____	2._____
3. _____	3. _____	3._____
4. _____	4. _____	4._____

5 *Marketing Media You Create on Your Own*

The external marketing tools described in this chapter—audiocassettes, videocassettes, newsletters, brochures and direct mail—have many uses and applications, which can be as varied and different as your own imagination allows. All of them, however, are tools that you actually deliver to your clients—through the mail, by hand or, in the case of audiotapes, even by phone. Unlike seminars or special events in which you directly communicate your message in person, these printed or recorded giveaways represent you to your target public. All of them are designed to expand your client base.

Although you may find that one or another tool or technique works particularly well for you, it's important to use a variety. To create a strong marketing presence usually requires combining a number of different external marketing approaches. For example, if your data base consists of 3,000 prospects and clients, all of them won't respond in the same way to the same marketing techniques. To maximize market penetration, you should make sure you have something that will appeal to every type of person or firm you target. External marketing often has a cumulative effect, too. Repeating your message in different forms gets a better response than simply hitting the target once.

DOOR OPENERS

Approaching your prospects in a unique way heightens the likelihood that they will retain a strong, positive impression and will remember you when a need arises for your services. Be bold in your approach. You'll need to take some risks, and perhaps you'll get some doors slammed, but remember, you don't need to turn every prospect into a client. There are many ways to entice your prospects into opening the door.

AUDIOCASSETTES

Audiocassettes can provide an exceptionally powerful communication and marketing tool—a tool that every financial professional should use. People appreciate audiocassettes because they add flexibility, and listening to them doesn't require much of a commitment of time or energy. Whereas many people feel that they don't have time to read, attend special presentations or even talk to you on the phone, they will often be more than willing to listen to a cassette during the otherwise dead commute time driving to or from work, for example, or while jogging or doing some other type of exercise. These people will value your acknowledging and accommodating their busy schedules in this way.

The audio format offers several marketing advantages. First, it gives you a more direct, personal way of touching your prospect than the use of printed material allows. While the audiotape tends to provide a more personal connection—similar in some respects to a face-to-face presentation—the listener has the option of turning it off or on at whim and has no obligation to respond. Cassettes tend to last longer than printed material due to their relatively high perceived value; people are less likely to throw them away than they would a flier or brochure. Last, recording and disseminating an audiotape of your own will make you different; you'll be providing your clients and prospects with something a little out of the ordinary, setting you apart from your competition.

Producing audiocassettes is relatively inexpensive, and they have a wide variety of uses. If you plan to use them to describe financial products, make sure that the information you present complies with the laws and regulations in effect in your state of practice.

VIDEOCASSETTES

Historically, videotapes have been among the more expensive external marketing tools to produce. The recent introduction of paperboard, rather than plastic, packaging, however, has significantly reduced the costs of videocassette production and mailing. Production costs as low as $1 per piece and third-class mailing as low as $.15 each can bring the videocassette well within even a conservative marketing budget.

In some cases, where audiocassettes are good, videocassettes can be even better. Since a videocassette has a high perceived value, many prospects are impressed by the effort and care that went into its production.

The major drawback to the videocassette is that the recipient will need to set aside a block of time specifically to watch it. An individual can listen to an audiocassette while doing something else (like driving, for instance). Watching a videocassette requires a commitment of time and interest. How can you encourage people to watch it? Two to three days after you send it to a prospect, try following up with a note and some popcorn!

IMAGE KITS AND BROCHURES

Developing a comprehensive image kit that reflects your style and quality of service is a critical component of any external marketing plan. Because you never get a second chance to make a good first impression, and because style communicates so much, you should be willing to invest adequate time and money in the preparation of your kit to make sure that you're conveying the image that's right for you. If you produce a package of materials that's well designed and somewhat unusual, it will communicate that you are a thoughtful, innovative professional and can offer creative ways to address your clients' needs.

Choose a conservative graphic style for your letterhead and business cards to promote your image, but base your choice of style on the area in which you do business and the tastes of your target market.

Here are some of the materials you should include in your kit:

- Letterhead and envelopes
- Business cards
- Self-adhesive (removable back) address labels
- Folders (for client presentations)
- Notepads

- "FYI" cards
- Image brochures

All of these materials should have a consistent look; they should share the same graphic design elements and be printed on matching paper stock using a complementary or identical color palette. All too often, this is an area that financial professionals don't take seriously enough. It's human nature to judge a book by its cover. As professional as you are, you need to make sure that your packaging makes you look that way to the world.

Within your image kit, your brochure occupies the highest position in marketing importance. As your primary calling card, it will introduce you to your market, reinforcing the good judgment of your new clients for having chosen you, and reeling in your undecided prospects.

DIRECT MAIL

Instead of cold calls, try making making warm calls. Send out an introductory letter, brochure, flier or invitation. Then call. That way, the person you're contacting may know who you are and may be more receptive.

You can use audiocassettes in conjunction with direct mail. Send an introductory letter describing your services and asking if the prospect is interested in receiving additional information by mail. If you get a positive response, send out your cassette—an unusual and effective approach that will make you different.

When you use direct mail, try sending out small, manageable mailings so that you can follow up with phone calls. Make sure that the direct mail piece is addressed to the right person. Wait to send the direct mail package to your best prospects until you've tested it thoroughly and have modified it based on your preliminary response.

NEWSLETTERS

Newsletters containing general-interest articles about the economy, tax and legal issues and investment ideas will significantly enhance your reputation as an expert and help position you as a media resource and industry leader. If it turns out to be a really good newsletter, you can charge for it. But even if you don't want to make subscribers pay for it, you can print a price on it anyway, which could increase its perceived value.

Many people hesitate to produce a newsletter because they are intimidated by what they fear will be an elaborate production process. It's not necessary, however, for a newsletter to be typeset or desktop-published, or even to be professionally printed. Often, just a simple typewritten "highlights" type of letter on your own business letterhead, photocopied in the quantity you require, will accomplish your goals equally as well as something more sophisticated. Again, you need to consider the tastes, style and sophistication of the prospects and clients you want to reach. As you collect interesting bits of information over time, such as quick investment planning ideas, tax or insurance tips or new product information, set them aside for a highlights letter. After you've collected enough items, put them together and you'll have a ready-made letter!

DOOR OPENERS

STRATEGY

38   BE CREATIVE WITH DOOR OPENERS

The essential ingredient in using these techniques successfully is a large measure of self-confidence.

⑤ *$100 bills.* Sid Friedman, a top insurance professional, has a novel way of making unscheduled visits to top executives. When they refuse to see him, as they typically do, he pulls two crisp, new $100 bills out of his wallet, gives them to the executive's secretary or assistant, and says "Give them to your boss, and tell him (or her) that I know his time is valuable. So if he agrees to see me and if after ten minutes he doesn't feel the time has been well spent, he can keep the $200." Of course, for you to use this technique, you have to be confident in your professional abilities and presentation skills. Friedman is (deservedly so), and he says the technique has provided him with more than enough business to compensate for the very few times he has had to leave the money behind. Because this approach is somewhat risky, we suggest that, if you try it, you use smaller sums of money—$100 or $50, for example.

⑤ *Unsigned checks.* A similar technique is used by Richard Kado in Edmonds, Washington, who sends unsigned checks to selected small business owners in his target area; each check is made out to the business owner for a certain dollar amount. In his cover letter, Kado asks for an appointment and promises, "If I can't save you at least twice the amount of this check, I'll sign it."

⑤ *Three-minute egg timers.* Robert Mark, a financial planner in White Plains, New York, sends three-minute egg timers to his key prospects with a letter requesting a few minutes of the prospects' time. The letter guarantees that the phone call will only take three minutes. The approach is so novel that when Mark follows up with the call, he often gets an appointment afterward. Remember, however, that if you promise your prospect a three-minute phone call, you need to be able to deliver on that promise. You should develop a number of key questions that underscore the need for your particular product or service and that also provide you with valuable information about the prospect.

⑤ *Candy.* Kevin Coyle of Consulting Research in Northfield, Illinois, uses the ERISA red book to build his list of prospects. He identifies likely targets by ZIP code and plan size, looking for small to medium-sized plans within particular local areas. After he develops a list, he verifies the addresses and uses a map to plan the most effective route to drop off his marketing packages. The package consists of a cover letter introducing his services, a brochure and a small box of attractively wrapped chocolate. When he arrives at one of the target firms, he says to the chief executive's receptionist, secretary or assistant, "I know that your boss's time is valuable, so I wanted to drop off this package for her (or him) to look at when she has time. I'll call again next week to see if I can answer any questions." And then, handing the assistant the box of chocolate, he says, "And this is for you for your trouble."

This technique provides a clever way to overcome what many consider to be the first obstacle to reaching an executive: the executive's assistant. It also provides Kevin a unique way to obtain the name of the executive if he doesn't already have it. As he's leaving, he asks the assistant, "By the way, what's the name of the person you're going to give this [the package] to?" He finds that the assistant never hesitates to tell him. As an alternative to candy, you could also try such gifts as flowers, a decorative pin or a scarf.

In 1989, Kevin delivered between 800 and 900 of his special marketing packages, and, of the firms he reached, 12 became clients—representing a signficant volume of new business.

39   To Improve Marketing Impact, Offer Something Free

Offering your prospects a "freebee" can often encourage your target prospects to open the door and will generally increase the response rate to your marketing efforts. An audiocassette, newsletter, brochure or pamphlet are just a few free items that you can promote. "Free" is a very powerful concept; you can use it to great advantage in turning prospects in many different markets into clients. As an example, try sending your prospects a certificate for a free 30-minute consultation. All giveaways should consist of professionally meaningful items (such as any of the examples listed above) in order to preserve the professional integrity of your marketing efforts. You should note, however, that using the word "free" may not always be appropriate in professional marketing. Some alternatives that you might choose instead are "complimentary," or "without cost."

40　Drip, Drip, Drip

Phil Broyles, a San Francisco–based professional sales trainer, strongly advocates using the "drip method" with your prospects, dripping at least six times before you quit. In other words, don't give up until you've established contact at least six different times. Keep dripping on those prospects. A drip can be a follow-up letter after meeting someone, a brochure, seminar invitation, newsletter, article reprint, audiocassette, or phone call.

[s] *Last-ditch drips.* For a final drip, consider mailing out a brief letter or questionnaire inquiring as to whether the client or prospect has any interest in continuing discussions/being called for an appointment; include a pre-addressed, postage-paid return envelope.

If, after six drips, there's still no response, you can almost always move on to greener marketing pastures. However, if the individual is a client, or a prospect who has at one time expressed an interest in your services, and you think he or she may just be procrastinating, try this last-ditch drip. Send the individual a telegram that says you've been expecting to hear from him or her and that you have some good ideas to share. This is an aggressive approach, and it may turn some people off—although if it does at this point you probably won't mind. On the other hand, others may respond positively and give you a call. You can be certain, at least, that anyone who receives such a telegram will read it. And, in any event, you have nothing to lose.

AUDIOCASSETTES

---

41   RECORD A SEMINAR

Send the audiocassette to the prospects and clients you invited to your seminar but who didn't attend, or send it to those individuals you forgot to invite. The people who were invited but didn't attend may very well have had a conflicting engagement, but would appreciate the opportunity to listen to the seminar on tape and would value your thoughtfulness in sending it to them. You could also send the cassette to the people who did attend; they may want to listen to your presentation again!

[S] *Recording another professional.* If another financial professional is presenting a particularly worthwhile seminar, get written permission to record it and send that cassette as well to your prospects and clients. They'll value the information and remember that you were the one who presented it to them, especially if you can place your own label on the tape.

[S] *Editing your cassette or "re-recording" your seminar.* After recording a live seminar, you can and should have the extraneous material edited out. Live presentations typically include visually oriented information that has little or no value to someone who's just listening to the tape and isn't part of the live audience. In addition, the recording may contain long pauses, throat-clearing, coughing and other noise that detracts from the value of the material being presented. Most unnecessary sounds can be removed through careful, professional editing. The only problem with doing this is that the recording may suffer some loss of quality. If the original recording is on a cassette, the tape needs to be transferred to a reel-to-reel master for editing; the edited tape is then transferred back into a cassette format, but this new cassette represents a second-generation recording—not the original recording made at the seminar itself.

One solution to the dilemma of obtaining a good-quality audiocassette is simply to record your seminar presentation in a professional recording studio. In this scenario, you would read your material from a prewritten script. You would then be able to offer the cassette as an alternative to attending the seminar—giving invitees the option of attending the seminar in person or purchasing the cassette. Many people, however, have a difficult time reading from a script in a studio. The lack of live audience feedback inhibits them and can make their performance less than what it would be at the actual seminar.

The solution that we like best represents a third option. Present the live seminar and record it. This audiocassette would be used just to transcribe your actual presentation—word for word. You would then review the transcript and clean it up as needed (to correct the mistakes in grammar, noun-verb agreement, etc., that we all make in speech). Using this slightly edited and much polished transcript, you would then create an original cassette recording in a studio. This method solves the problem of sound quality, since you'd be making a first-generation recording. It also virtually guarantees that you'll be recording a good presentation; if your seminar was good, the tape should be good too, since your studio script will be practically identical to that of your live performance. It will still contain your words, your syntax and your intonation.

42   RECORD THE FIRST INTERVIEW WITH A CLIENT

This can be a highly valuable tool for both you and the client. Record the initial interview and then give a copy of the audiocassette to the client. Relatively inexpensive cassette recorders with tape duplicating capabililty are available. Let's face it: Both you and your client may not remember or may not have fully understood or even heard all the points discussed during the interview. The cassette will allow both of you the opportunity to easily review all the information exchanged during the meeting and, consequently, could help the client make easier and better informed investment decisions at the next meeting. This technique works particularly well for elderly clients. It will also provide useful background material for your assistant or casewriter who later interacts with the client.

STRATEGY

43   Record a Description of Your Own Business

This type of audiocassette can become a part of your calling card, something you can leave behind with, or send to, a new client or prospect. Keep it brief—no longer than eight to 12 minutes. If you find that you need much more time to tell your story, consider making a second tape or a series of tapes to send to your prospects in a timed sequence. The cassette, or series of tapes, can stand alone as your corporate brochure, or you can use it to accompany and supplement the other printed materials that describe your services. For this type of cassette, it's best to use a professional recording studio and to let one of your peers critique the trial runs.

S *Recording an interview of yourself by a local media star.* Consider hiring a local radio, TV or newspaper personality to interview you on tape; you can write or edit the script yourself to tell your story. This format is attractive because it's different and communicates in a more interesting way. One note of caution, however, in hiring a professional media personality. You must make it clear to your listeners that the media personality has been hired by you. You should explain at the beginning of the audio program that the interviewer's purpose is solely to moderate the discussion or interview, which you've prepared in advance to describe your business, and that the program doesn't constitute his or her endorsement of your services.

S *Including your audiocassette in your image kit.* You can include your cassette in your media or marketing kit, and use it when you solicit speaking engagements. If the organization you're soliciting the engagement from doesn't know anything about you, this will provide them with some valuable information. It will also reinforce your image as a speaker and chances are it will distinguish you from all the other speakers who are soliciting the same opportunity.

---

44   CREATE AN AUDIO NEWSLETTER

An audio newsletter will give you a way to maintain a close, personal relationship with many of your clients and prospects with a very small commitment of time. And again, it's unique.

Some people just don't like to read; others don't have time. If you already produce a printed newsletter, you can produce an audio version as well and give your audience the choice of which they'd like to receive. Just as printed newsletters feature guest columnists from time to time, your audio newsletter could feature guest speakers or regular commentators who could present specialized information on any number of different topics of interest.

45   TAPE A PRODUCT WHOLESALER OR SPONSOR

When someone comes into your office to do an investment presentation, get permission to tape it. You can archive the cassette in your library and use it later for quick reference as well as for your own client presentations. Stockbrokers may also be able to record presentations of lesser-known companies launching initial public offerings to use with those clients contemplating an IPO stock purchase.

46 RECORD AN INFORMATIONAL MESSAGE ON YOUR ANSWERING MACHINE

If you use an answering machine at your office, you can record and periodically update an outgoing message that contains tax tips, investment advice, your views on a current economic situation or other
information that callers might find useful. The message might even
elicit calls from people wanting information who might not otherwise
be inclined to contact you. After the informative message, the recording could conclude with something like, "If you'd like additional information, or if you'd like to talk to X, Y or Z, please leave your name
and number after the tone." Allan Feldman, a financial planner in
Scottsdale, Arizona, uses this effective technique to generate leads and
calls it "Tip from the Top." Use a specialized business card or run
small newspaper ads to publicize the service. Don't forget to promote
your telephone message service in your newsletters and seminars too.

47   DEVELOP AN EDUCATIONAL PROGRAM ON TAPE

Like a seminar series, these audiocassettes could provide educational opportunities on key financial topics. You could sell them individually and package them collectively as a series, promoting them in your newsletter, in ads and in live seminars that you offer to the public. The cost to the consumer could be relatively low. The public would receive an educational bargain, and you would establish yourself as an important informational resource.

Generic financial topics for this type of treatment might include the following:

- How to maximize profits from selling your home: the six key points to remember
- The critical areas to include in your will, and how to avoid probate
- Seven impediments to successful investing
- Financial planning considerations for your career or job change
- Twelve ways to reduce taxes
- Tips to obtain a new home mortgage
- Setting and achieving financial goals
- Pros and cons of the five most common investments

Although preparing a series of educational cassettes will involve some work and expense, it will provide you with an unusually attractive promotional vehicle.

VIDEOCASSETTES

---

48   USE VIDEOS TO ILLUSTRATE INVESTMENT OPPORTUNITIES

You can present videocassettes on various investment opportunities to select clients. Wholesalers will often provide you with the cassettes, which you can pass along to your clientele. When you give a client a videotape, ask him or her to return it to you; better yet, drop by to pick it up and use that opportunity to make an appointment.

49   Use Videos To Market Your Practice

Some people who are too busy to talk to you may appreciate receiving a videocassette that describes who you are and the range of services you offer. You can use it in tandem with, or in place of, a printed marketing brochure. Unlike a brochure, a videocassette leaves the door open for a second contact with the prospect since you have to get back in touch in order to retrieve the cassette.

---

50   VIDEOTAPE YOUR SEMINAR

In certain circumstances, you may find that a videotape of your seminar will have greater value than an audiocassette. If, for instance, your
seminar relies heavily on visual materials—statistical graphs, charts
and drawings—video will be the most meaningful way of recording the
presentation. Consider sending your client an audiocassette and transcript too, in addition to the videotape, so that the client has a choice
and can select the medium he or she prefers.

[s] *Including a video within your seminar.* For an interesting twist,
you can enliven a seminar by introducing a videotaped presentation as
part of your own presentation. The videotape could be a short presentation by another financial professional or by an expert in another, unrelated firm communicating information that tied into your seminar
material.

IMAGE KITS AND BROCHURES

---

51 PROMOTE YOUR OWN NAME

If you're in business for yourself, it's preferable to use your name for the company—like Edward Rose & Associates, for example—rather than a generic business name (such as "Financial Resources, Inc.") that doesn't have anything to do with you personally. You are, after all, what makes your business successful, and you want people to remember who you are. Generic names are often difficult for people to remember. The Coca-Cola Company can afford to spend the millions of dollars necessary to effectively promote its generic name. Chances are, you can't.

[S] *Nicknames.* In certain markets and situations, giving yourself a nickname can often make you more memorable to your clients, prospects and centers of influence. In the early 1970s, we worked with a lot of people in real estate, but, in truth, we only remember a few. One of them is Barry Friedlander who works for RE/MAX in Boulder, Colorado. We remember him because he goes by the name "Bear." No one forgets him because the name is unusual—particularly within the context of a professional business setting. We also recall a broker named "Hoot" Gibson; after all, how could we forget the name of one of the cowboy stars of our youth?

52   MAKE YOUR BROCHURE SIMPLE, BUT ELEGANT

Your brochure should be comprehensive, but brief. Designing it to fit in a letter-size envelope can result in major cost savings because you'll be able to enclose it with prospecting letters in a compact format.

[s] *Making it professional.* Your brochure is one of the most personal representations of the quality of work you do—not just as a marketer of your own services, but much more importantly, as a provider of the services themselves. Give your brochure the same level of attention that you would give to a client.

Although creating a brochure can be expensive, don't try to cut too many corners. The content and form of the brochure you end up with will be projecting your image, and it's essential that your image convey your professionalism, your expertise and the high quality of your services. It's important enough to go first-class, so look to communications professionals—small advertising agencies, independent graphic artists and writers—to help you develop a brochure that will meet your needs.

It's usually a good idea for the brochure to contain a die-cut pocket, either on the inside back cover or, if the brochure has three panels on each side, on the middle panel. You can use the pocket for information that belongs in your brochure but that may periodically become dated. These materials might include the following:

- Profiles of your firm's employees, consisting of brief biographical sketches that your clients and prospects might find interesting
- Your fee schedules
- Reprints of articles you've written or in which you've been quoted
- Reference lists of people who work for you, including other financial professionals (attorneys, bankers, accountants, bookkeepers, etc.)
- Reference lists of satisfied clients with whom you've worked, perhaps including several testimonial letters
- Special calendars of events

Even if you're a stockbroker, for example, you can include a fee schedule for your firm as well as a separate schedule if you do additional independent consulting work. You might even include a form that shows how you evaluate a client's portfolio when you make stock recommendations. A financial planner could include a sample plan document to show clients and prospects how the planning process works.

Printing materials such as these separately and including them as inserts creates a modular system that allows you to update your brochure cost-effectively, extending its life; when data become obsolete, you can simply reprint the appropriate insert card(s) rather than the entire brochure. All of the inserts you include should be designed and printed in a compatible format to complement the look of the brochure.

Don't forget to include your address and telephone number somewhere on your brochure. (Believe it or not, some people actually forget these essentials!)

[s] *Avoiding industry jargon.* As financial services professionals, we often tend to get caught up in our own jargon. We sometimes overlook the fact that our clients and potential clients aren't necessarily that sophisticated. Speak to them in language they can understand, eliminating industry lingo as much as possible. Stress results rather than try to explain your process. Communicate the benefits a client will receive from working with you. Use what J. William Mize, CPA, calls "power phrases." As examples:

- "Accumulate wealth without increasing your earnings."
- "Use inflation to your advantage."
- "Keep more of what you earn."
- "Make more of your money work harder for you."
- "Avoid being among the vast number of Americans who are broke at age 65."

Good writers will tell you that phrases such as these are particularly effective because they speak in terms of "user benefits."

[s] *Proofreading.* Because your brochure is critical in promoting your professional image, something as insignificant as a typo can create dire results. Take the time to examine the galley proofs (or desktop-

published output) carefully before sending your artwork to press. If you don't feel comfortable doing this yourself, hire a skilled proofreader to do it for you. Investing a few dollars in this essential component of production can often make a world of difference between looking like a success and looking silly.

[S] *Printing more than you think you'll need.* Let the agency or graphic artist you choose help you select a high-quality paper stock for your brochure. It will cost a little more, but will further enhance the image of high quality and stability that you want to project.

Most often, printing larger quantities will result in significant per-piece cost savings for you. You'll find, for example, that printing a quantity of 5,000 brochures won't cost that much more than printing 2,500, so consider going with the higher quantity; not only will your per-piece cost be less, but it's always cheaper to print extras at the outset than to go back to the printer later to reprint small quantities.

[S] *Printing two versions.* By the same token, if you're targeting more than one market segment, you might choose to alter the brochure copy slightly so that you can have a second brochure that specifically addresses that second target. If the brochures are identical except for some differences in the copy, you'll also realize significant savings by printing them both at the same time. To the printer, both brochures will essentially represent one printing run; and with the exception of the small charge for making a new plate for the second brochure and the additional quantity of brochures required, there shouldn't be any additional charges.

This recommendation holds true for your "specialty" brochure as well. If you decide to specialize in a particular area in addition to your general practice or service, this would be an opportune time to create a brochure describing the new service, printing it at the same time that you print your brochure for your general practice.

DIRECT MAIL

53 MAIL IT TWICE

Often, the response from the second mailing is equal to or even greater than the response from the first. People tend to put mail aside or just throw it away. The second mailing serves as a reminder to them. Just think about the mail-order catalogs you receive. One week you'll receive the spring catalog from a manufacturer of sports apparel, for example; a week later, you'll receive the *same* catalog—this time with a different cover! Interestingly, more people order merchandise from this second catalog than they do from the first.

You can get mailing lists from a variety of sources: clubs, business directories in your local library, associations, the Yellow Pages and mail service houses (by ZIP code if you like).

54   MAKE SURE IT GETS THEIR ATTENTION

The flier or literature needs to have an attention-grabbing device so that the recipients will want to read it and find out what it's about. This device can be a graphic design element that encourages the reader to open the flier or envelope (to see what's inside), or it can manifest itself through a nuance in the copy appearing on the cover, similarly enticing the reader to go on and discover more.

An example of an introductory sentence "grabber" might be "I can probably save you more in taxes in the next 12 months than you put into savings last year." Obviously, this is an aggressive approach. You can be less aggressive in your copy platform; you simply need to capture the reader's attention. Hire an ad agency or independent graphic artist to help you develop strong copy and an effective design. Keep the copy brief and to the point.

[s] *Making it personal.* If you use an envelope for your direct mail piece, the following techniques will increase the likelihood that the recipient will open it up.

- For seminars, use a non-business-size envelope (greeting card sizes work well).
- Address the envelope by hand; calligraphy or easy-to-read script are equally effective.
- Make sure there's nothing on the outside of the envelope that indicates that it has a business purpose.
- Use commemorative postage stamps.
- Mark the envelope "personal."

[s] *Including a message of urgency and a way to respond.* Create a deadline for people to respond to the solicitation. This helps prevent them from filing the flier away with the vague intention to act on it later. Including a perforated, postage-paid business reply card is best. The object is to make it as easy as possible for the recipients to respond.

The business reply card ought to be easy to read and simple to fill out. It should be printed on a non-gloss paper stock, which is much easier to write on and to read than glossy stock, and it should provide ample space to fill in the requested information. For seniors, the type size should be relatively large since many older people have poor eyesight.

With luck, the business reply card will be mailed back to you. The client may, however, keep the remaining portion of the flier for later reference. Make sure that you have your name, address and telephone number on it! (Note, on the direct mail solicitations you yourself receive, how often this obvious rule is overlooked.)

If you wish to obtain more information from your prospects than can comfortably fit on a card, develop a separate form and include in your outgoing mailing a pre-addressed, postage-paid envelope so that they can easily return the form to you.

s *Including something they can keep.* You can also incorporate into your flier a business card or Rolodex card that your targets can tear off and keep. An item like this gives prospects an easy way to keep you "on file" for future reference.

---

55   SEND IT FIRST CLASS

Postage is a substantial expense, but too often people try to cut corners by sending direct mail bulk rate, with unfortunate results. The worst thing that can happen is for the mail to arrive later than the seminar or meeting date described in the flier, or later than the deadline required for a response. First-class postage provides much better protection against potential delays.

People disagree, however, as to which type of postage is more cost-effective in soliciting a response. If you have plenty of time (and don't mind some of the fliers taking up to three or more weeks to reach their destinations), try sending some of the fliers bulk rate, or using a third-class stamp, and others first class to see whether the actual level of response differs.

⑤ *Postal regulations.* The U.S. Postal Service has some fairly restrictive rules concerning the design and printing of direct mail and business reply mail materials. If you're working with an ad agency or graphic design firm, have them check to make sure that the flier design conforms to the regulations before it goes to press. If you're designing the piece yourself, you can get a copy of the regulations from a local post office. The restrictions concern paper weight for self-mailers and business reply cards, as well as the specific placement of copy on the address side of the flier and reply card. Failure to comply can result in the Postal Service's refusal to process and deliver your mail.

⑤ *Direct mail services.* You can find numerous mail houses and direct mail fulfillment services that are set up expressly to handle large-volume mailings. If you plan a mailing to more than, say, 5,000 target recipients, using a letter service may be more cost-effective in the time it will save you than your doing it yourself. Mail houses offer a great deal of flexibility in the way in which they will work with you, depending on your particular needs and objectives.

STRATEGY

56   BE DIFFERENT

All it takes is a little imagination and, sometimes, the willingness to take a little risk. Here are several unique concepts that may work for you too.

⑤ *Thanksgiving cards.* Barbara DiPalma, a financial planner in Spring Valley, New York, sends Thanksgiving cards to her clients. A traditional nonsectarian holiday that everyone celebrates, Thanksgiving provides her an opportunity to express thanks for her clients' business. Since no one else sends Thanksgiving cards, the gesture makes her unique.

⑤ *Graphic illustrations of investment products.* Robert Coe, a Boston stockbroker, sends the letter shown in Figure 5–1 to his clientele and hot prospects. Notice the attention-getting graphic and response vehicle. Coe maintains a data base of approximately 130,000 individuals from whom his other direct mail efforts typically get an average one percent to one and one-half percent response. This letter, however, with its powerful graphic statement, typically obtains a four percent response.

⑤ *"Valu-Pak" coupon stuffers.* One broker we heard about in Teaneck, New Jersey, uses a well-researched coupon service for shotgun marketing in his area, a strategy that has yielded great success. On a quarterly basis, he produces his coupon ad, which includes a business reply card inviting the reader to come in for a free investment portfolio analysis. His ad is stuffed into an envelope marked "valuable coupons" with ads for approximately 20 to 30 other local businesses and sent to some 180,000 residences and businesses in the area. The ad results in approximately 800 to 900 responses; of those, some 50 percent become clients.

⑤ *Letters to newborn children.* W. Douglas O'Rear in Brentwood, Tennessee, sends letters to newborn babies (not to their parents), welcoming them to the world and suggesting that it's never too soon to begin planning for a college education. He looks for notices of recent births in local newspaper announcements and also in records at the county courthouse. His letter offers a free consultation and a silver spoon for the baby when the family comes in to his office—a clever marketing approach that has worked well for this financial planner.

⬛S *Letters to seminar attendees.* James N. Reardon, J.D., a certified financial planner with Clayton Financial Services in Topeka, Kansas, assembles a mailing list of the business owners who have attended his seminars and then sends them the letter seen in Figure 5-2.

Reardon typically gets a 50 percent response to his assistant's calls inviting the business owners to lunch. Of these, one-third become clients, and another third generate referrals and future business.

Figure 5-1. Investment Promotion Letter

You have seen this bar code on many products, but you haven't seen anything yet. Soon library books, automobile parts, and most equipment manufactured for the armed services will be bar coded. The bar code system for inventory control and point of sales records is fast, efficient, and accurate. The cost savings for users is tremendous.

One company in this fast growing industry has a 90% market share of the hand-held laser scanning guns used to read bar codes. Sales of this company have expanded from 3.5 million in 1983 to 90 million dollars in 1988. Sales for the year ending December 1989 are estimated to be 240 million !! The market for bar code scanning equipment should grow from 150 million in 1986 to over 1.5 billion in 1991. We expect this company to grow at an annual rate of 35% for the next five years.

If you are interested in finding out more about this rapidly growing company, please return this letter or a business card in the enclosed postage paid envelope. For more rapid service, feel free to call me using our toll free number.

Very truly yours,

Robert H. Coe

MASS 800–649–5608
USA 800–343–7068

Reprinted courtesy of Robert H. Coe.

Figure 5–2.   Letter to Seminar Attendees

Dear [Business Owner]:

Our research suggests that you, or your business, might benefit from the services of a registered investment advisory firm. In fact, *Businessweek* magazine reports that as many as 30 million people could use the services of a competent financial advisory firm.

If all 30 million of these people were *aware* of this need, I probably wouldn't be sending this letter. The fact is that most people do not yet know how to use a registered investment advisory firm effectively. They often tend to equate our services with those already being provided by their attorney, accountant, stockbroker, life insurance agent, real estate broker, financial planner, psychologist, spouse or bartender.

While the principals in our firm have some combined experience or credentials in *all* of these professions, our major focus is on financial services that are unique to our firm. That's why our clients include members of all the above professions, plus bankers, physicians, dentists, psychiatrists, electricians and plumbers. We also provide services to

- Pension and profit-sharing plans
- Trusts and fiduciaries
- Nonprofit and charitable organizations
- Trade unions and teacher groups
- Corporations and sole proprietorships
- Large and small investors

In the past few months we have been quoted by *Money* magazine, *Parenting* magazine and the *Topeka Capital Journal*. We have prepared workshops and educational seminars for more than 30 professional and trade associations, two of the city's largest employers, and for Washburn University's continuing education department and Emporia State University.

We would like to have the opportunity to perhaps serve you at some time in the future. In a few days, I will call to invite you to be my luncheon guest at the Top of the Tower Club. At that time I would like to give you a brief summary of our services and a quick tour of our eighth-floor offices in Bank IV Tower.

I sincerely hope that you will accept this opportunity to get acquainted with our firm.

Courtesy James N. Reardon, Clayton Financial Group (Topeka, KS).

NEWSLETTERS

STRATEGY

57   USE YOUR NEWSLETTER FOR COMMUNITY AWARENESS

Think of your newsletter as a periodic letter to your clients updating and advising them on important financial events and opportunities, and providing them with interesting bits of information. You can use it for bulletins and notices, financial tips, predictions and observations.

⑤ *Neighborhood newsletters.* One financial planner has developed a newsletter specifically for her residential neighborhood. She includes a classified advertising section and provides general information about the area that her neighbors really appreciate—which houses are for sale, for instance, and average home sales prices—as well as financially applicable news. This strategy is a proven winner for garnering referrals.

⑤ *Including a glossary in your newsletter.* This would consist of special terms and concepts that pertain to your target market. Often, clients and prospects don't understand certain investment concepts or aren't even aware of them. Publishing a glossary will help educate your market while demonstrating your specialization.

---

58   PUBLISH IT AS A JOINT UNDERTAKING

To save money and time, you can create a newsletter in tandem with another financial professional, or with several other professionals. Consider collaborating with a local college economics professor who could supply you with a regular column of economic commentary. The professor would most likely charge a fee, but the cost might be small in comparison to the credibility you would gain by having your own consulting economist.

[S] *Using other companies' newsletters.* One financial planner we heard from tells us that writing articles for other companies' employee newsletters works well. Sometimes these newsletters can also be used to run ads.

[S] *Using ad agencies or writers.* A common complaint among professionals about newsletter publication is that they just don't have the time it takes to produce one on a regular basis. One solution is to hire someone to produce it for you. With your input and direction, an independent writer or firm can handle every component of the process—from writing the articles through layout, pasteup and printing, saving you valuable time and assuring you of a professional, well-written and well-designed product. Desktop publishing software has additionally made newsletter publication a lot easier and less expensive than in the past. But, again, if you don't have the time or in-house writing or graphic design capabilities yourself, look to professionals for assistance.

STRATEGY

59   SEND IT OUT AT LEAST QUARTERLY

Regularity is key. Keep reminding your newsletter audience that you have a lot of information to share with them. Start with a quarterly newsletter; then try publishing it bimonthly or monthly. If it gets good enough, you might be able to sell it to other financial professionals who would use their own masthead for it and perhaps add a personalized article or two of their own.

You might consider writing most of your first *two* issues even before you send out the first one just to stay ahead of the game. If certain columns in the newsletter are kept generic enough, you'll always be able to write them ahead of time, and you'll then have a smaller portion of the newsletter devoted to current issues or events, making it easier to write.

60 SEND IT OUT TO THE WORLD

If you spend some time creating a valuable newsletter, don't hesitate to share the wealth; it will only reflect well on you.

[s] *Prospective and existing clients.* Like educational seminars or audiocassettes, newsletters are an effective way to keep your target market informed and to promote your services without a face-to-face interview. From time to time, test the usefulness of including a coupon, to be clipped and returned to you, requesting more information on a particular product, service or piece of information in the newsletter. You can position the coupon in such a way that when it's cut out, the client's or prospect's address label will be on the other side.

[s] *Sending additional copies.* If the newsletter contains general-interest articles, your clients may very well pass it along to associates, relatives or friends who might be interested. In fact, why not send them a second copy with a specific suggestion to pass it along? If you do this, be sure to include in the newsletter a highlighted message that lets readers know that they can receive their own subscription by phoning or by sending in a special coupon that can be clipped from the newsletter. You should, of course, maintain ample supplies of your newsletter. While the extra printing costs will be nominal, the potential for client referrals will be great.

[s] *Other financial professionals.* Send your newsletter to CPAs, attorneys, insurance brokers, and other financial professionals with whom you network. Some of the information may be useful to them, and the newsletter will help keep your name in their minds. Send your newsletter to the media as well to position yourself as an educational and quotable resource in your community.

TO GET STARTED...

Of all the new strategies you've found in this chapter, which one would you most like to implement in each of the following categories?

1. Audiocassettes _____
2. Videocassettes _____
3. Image kits and brochures _____
4. Direct mail _____
5. Newsletters _____
6. List any additional strategies that occurred to you as you were reading the chapter. _____
7. Choose any two of the strategies listed above that you'd like to try. Identify the steps you'll need to take to implement them.

Strategy: _____

Implementation Steps:	Date To Complete:	Who Will Implement the Steps If Not You?
1. _____	1. _____	1._____
2. _____	2. _____	2._____
3. _____	3. _____	3._____
4. _____	4. _____	4._____

Strategy: _____

Implementation Steps:	Date To Complete:	Who Will Implement the Steps If Not You?
1. _____	1. _____	1._____
2. _____	2. _____	2._____
3. _____	3. _____	3._____
4. _____	4. _____	4._____

6 *Advertising and Public Relations*

Although advertising and public relations are primary external marketing tools, they are quite different from the other external marketing tools we've described in the preceding two chapters. Advertising and public relations require that you work with the existing media, developing your strategies to conform to their specific formats and rules. Accordingly, you don't have quite as much freedom of expression as you do, for instance, when you create your own brochure, cassette or direct mail flier. Nonetheless, the news media offer a very broad umbrella for projecting an image and, as such, are important components of any good marketing program.

ADVERTISING

Although advertising can be a costly undertaking, particularly for a small business or sole practitioner, a well thought-out ad program can yield meaningful results. If you decide to advertise, remember that frequency is almost always the most important factor. It's better, for example, to run a small ad consecutively in each issue, or in every other issue, of a local newspaper over a period of several months, rather than to "splash" a large ad just once or twice. In establishing an advertising program, you'll also need to test your market geographically as well as by your specialized target to see where the areas of greatest responsiveness and cost-benefits lie.

As you run a series of ads over a period of time, make sure that you keep the ad format the same, even if you change the message. This allows the reader, listener or viewer to readily identify and remember your service or firm.

Remember the value of the word "free." You may want to include a limited-time-offer coupon for a videocassette or audiocassette, free seminar tickets or consultation in order to stimulate reader response.

PUBLIC RELATIONS

Perhaps one of the least understood—and, therefore least used—marketing tools is P.R. Yet in many ways it is the most powerful marketing tool of all. Press exposure establishes credibility that can't be bought. Being quoted in the media or getting an article published not only generates immediate inquiries, but the reprint value has a very long life. Articles or news reprints make valuable additions to your marketing kit and direct mail.

The key to public relations is that *you* make it happen. Unless you have celebrity status, the media won't come to you; you have to go to them, and you have to convince them that you're a source of newsworthy information. Try to get a face-to-face meeting with the reporter of the local newspaper or the radio announcer of a station that features financial information to discuss ways in which you can supply him or her with information. Editors are always on the prowl for valuable sources of news and topical commentary. Call or write to them to arrange a meeting in which you explain your background and relate your expertise to their needs. If you write to them, include one of your newsletters. Editors like to receive materials like this, so you should make a point of adding them to your mailing list. Note too that your first contact with them will be most productive if you have at least one newsworthy idea to share.

Get to know what your target media are looking for and the styles that they like; if you can give them good information, they'll come back to you again and again. If you discover an error or inaccurate information that they've printed, point it out to them in a cordial letter. Editors usually want to know when they're wrong. Show them you're an expert in your profession and a reliable source of information.

Even if you don't have a story at the time of your first meeting, you can always follow up later with interesting information that readers or listeners might value. Remember this, however: As with anyone else, editors change jobs, so don't assume that the same editor you worked with two years ago still holds the same job today. If you become a good media resource, your name will be passed along from editor to editor, but it's a good practice to call ahead to verify the presence of a particular staff member before you send him or her information. A word of caution regarding the press: Here's a lesson Donald Trump learned the hard way. While the press can cheer you on during good times, understand that once they know who you are they are more likely to "turn on the heat" during difficult times.

As you develop a rapport with the local media, prepare your staff to be highly responsive when they call. Try not to keep them waiting for you. If they're working to meet a deadline and you're not available, you'll miss the opportunity to be quoted because they'll move on to call their second-best contact. Tell your assistant to put the call through to you regardless of whom you're with. Almost any client or prospect will be happy to excuse you for a few minutes, and will be suitably impressed, when he or she learns that you're dealing with the press.

ADVERTISING

61   TESTIMONIALS MAKE POWERFUL ADS

Mark Negless, a CFP with Private Ledger Financial Services in Vancouver, Washington, alternates product and testimonial ads twice weekly in his local newspaper, a method he has found to be one of the most effective types of print advertising available. He operates under the premise that his best new clients are "clones" of his existing clients. Negless asks his favorite clients to write a brief testimonial for him. He only asks those clients he knows very well and with whom he feels most comfortable. He tells them that he is developing a promotional piece for his business that will explain what he does as a financial planner; if the clients are satisfied with his service, would they write a brief paragraph on why he helps them with their finances?

"You tell your clients that you'll send them a letter, with a postage-paid return envelope, so they can write a paragraph on why they do business with you," says Negless. "Note that you don't have to call the paragraph a 'testimonial'; you just indicate that it may be used in a promotional piece. Be sure to thank them for their kindness."

"Upon receipt of the testimonial (and assuming that you like it), ask your client if you can use the letter in an ad, in which you would credit them by first name and last initial only, with their working status and residential location—for example, 'Grant and Bonnie P., retired, Portland, Oregon.' Whether or not they agree to allow you to include their testimonial in your ad, make sure that you always follow up with a thank-you note.

"If you've done a good job for your client," Negless maintains, "the client will feel honored to have you use the testimonial in an ad."

Negless suggests acquiring at least five of these testimonials before beginning the ad campaign, then rotating the ads weekly, highlighting one strong quotation in each testimonial with large boldface type (see Figure 6–1).

In his experience, Negless has received a more positive response to this kind of advertising than to any other he has used. The personal

Figure 6-1. Testimonial Ads

July 31 (Sunday)

"We have been very pleased

with Mark Negless's service on our retirement investments. He has thoroughly explained our options and has shown concern for our needs. He has contributed helpful suggestions and advice concerning budgeting our income to meet these needs now, and in the future."

— Ralph & Ardis, retired, Vancouver, WA

August 1 (Monday)

Mark Negless, CFP
1220 Main, Suite 475
Vancouver, WA 98660   **(206) 693-3355**

Markam G. Negless
Certified Financial Planner

Registered Securities Principal, Titan Value Equities. Member SIPC

August 7 (Sunday)

"Mark genuinely cares"

"I have been greatly encouraged and impressed by Mark's knowledge and professionalism in the handling of my financial matters. But more importantly to me, I believe Mark genuinely cares about people's personal needs. A trust that is personal, I feel, exists in our business relationship."

— Eldin, retired, Vancouver, WA

August 8 (Monday)

Mark Negless, CFP
1220 Main, Suite 475
Vancouver, WA 98660   **(206) 693-3355**

Markam G. Negless
Certified Financial Planner

Registered Securities Principal, Titan Value Equities. Member SIPC.

August 14 (Sunday)

"As a retired widow

I can't afford to speculate or take chances. I want security for my funds as well as a monthly income. Mr. Negless understands my position and found investments tailored to my personal needs. His patient explanations and willingness to find the answers to my particular financial problems make me feel he is a friend as well as an investment counselor."

—Eleanor, retired, Beaverton, OR

August 15 (Monday)

Mark Negless, CFP
1220 Main, Suite 475
Vancouver, WA 98660   **(206) 693-3355**

Markam G. Negless
Certified Financial Planner

Registered Securities Principal, Titan Value Equities. Member SIPC.

Courtesy of Markham G. Negless, CFP.

quality of the testimonials tends to attract potential clients because the ads strike a sympathetic chord in the reader.

"I think that when your prospects read an existing client's testimonial, they understand how your service will actually help them. This is true especially when they see that your client is retired, like they are. Or your client is a business owner, like they are. Or an airline pilot, like they are."

For a campaign like this, it might prove worthwhile to hire a graphics design firm to create a basic design format for the first ad. You could then substitute the copy with different testimonials as needed. Advertising typically produces the best results when you offer your target market consistency—in the overall look of the ads as well as the frequency with which they appear in print.

62   Share Advertising Costs

Consider sharing advertising costs with other professionals. Mary Vizioli, a REALTOR® Associate with Stephens Associates, Century 21 in Denville, New Jersey, cooperates with agents from competing firms to advertise to the same neighborhood. This enables her to get the full benefit of print advertising at a fraction of the cost. Although the houses that are for sale are jointly listed in the ads, each agent acts independently to show the property that he or she represents.

She takes the idea one step further: each of the agents refers prospective customers to the other's Open Houses.

You might also find it worthwhile to create a cooperative ad with a group of other financial professionals with whom you network. This provides a good way to spread out some of the costs of advertising and creates a generic source of financially oriented services that represents a very appealing package to the consumer. See Strategy 73 for a similar idea that would apply more directly to financial professionals.

63   Don't Overlook the Yellow Pages

Design and buy space for at least a small display ad in the Yellow Pages
that focuses on your area of specialization or general service. It's inexpensive, and people often look through the Yellow Pages when they
need to find a particular service or product. Having a well-designed,
well-conceived ad will make you visible here too.

STRATEGY

64   CONSIDER AN "ADVERTORIAL"

This is an advertisement that has a distinctly editorial flavor. It is essentially an editorial (or article) containing financial information; the difference is that you pay the newspaper or magazine to run it, and the word "advertisement" appears at the top of the column. You could, for instance, run an advertorial on how to pick a high-growth stock, why most people fail to save or how to determine how much insurance you need. A series of well-written educational (not self-promotional) advertorials will build strong credibility for you in your community. Including a very brief (one-line), low-key invitation to your services at the bottom of the ad—including your name, address and phone number—should generate leads.

⬚S⬚ *Positioning it well.* For print ads targeted to seniors, try requesting that your newspaper ad be placed next to the obituaries. This spot is not in very high demand, but just consider the market segment most likely to read the obituaries—seniors.

---

65   TRY A NEWSPAPER INSERT

This novel idea comes from George Bates in Rockford, Illinois. Every quarter, he produces a special four-page newspaper insert called "Money Matters" that gets inserted into a special weekly "Neighbors" section of the *Rockford Register Star*. Over a four-week period, the insert reaches the newspaper's entire readership of approximately 110,000, being distributed on a zone-by-zone basis that the planner directs.

The insert contains practical information on a wide variety of financially oriented topics designed to appeal to the public at large. The first insert (Figure 6–2) featured articles on the following topics:

- Year-end tax planning
- When to change an investment strategy
- Protecting against a major liability lawsuit
- How to determine a real rate of return

Believing that comprehensive financial planning requires the combined knowledge and experience of different professionals, Bates included articles from a CPA, a lawyer and an insurance specialist.

The insert program has been a huge success, generating new business for the financial planning firm and a tremendous awareness of its services within the community—among consumers and other professionals alike. Further, the financial professionals who have contributed specialized articles have also obtained impressive results, acquiring new clients and prospects themselves as a result of the broad-based exposure.

Figure 6–2. Money Matters Newspaper Insert

MONEY MATTERS

Courtesy of **Bates Financial Services**

Meet the Bates professionals

Debut issue of Money Matters

Dear Reader:

This is the first edition of a quarterly publication with the expressed desire of providing facts, opinions and views that you can use in your financial affairs.

We shall attempt to provide practical information that can help you in a wide variety of areas... for example planning for retirement, college education costs, income taxes, estate planning, insurance of various kinds.

It is our opinion that any serious attempt to cover these topics requires the knowledge and experience of several different professions, thus we will regularly include articles written by other professionals i.e. accountants, attorneys, insurance people. I can assure you that each contributing ~~author~~ ~~will~~ ~~need to express~~ ~~hi~~

Front Row: Donna Tomlinson, Cheryl Ross, Marilyn Knuth.
Back Row: Patrick Hermann, Rhoda Mabus, Charles H. Stephenson, Brent Brodeski, George E. Bates.

Bates Financial Services is an independent group of companies in the financial services business. We have an NASD (National Association of Securities Dealers) ~~license~~ ~~to~~ ~~selling~~ ~~investm~~ and nursing home insurance.

Though the Bates companies officially opened in Rockford in 1982, George E. Bates CFP, the President, has been involved in ~~more~~ ~~th~~ ~~five~~ ~~ye~~

cial professional becomes a necessary and valuable advisor.

We recommend a fundamental approach to investing with sound economic value, leaving fads and exotic investment to others.

Our approach to financial planning is that it is a process not an event and that process has five very important steps:

1) Identify the goals and objectives of the individual.

2) Take a complete financial inventory and determine the individual's attitude concerning risk, taxes, inflation, diversification, liquidity and flexibility.

3) Analyze the individual's situation and design a financial plan that will help attain the stated goals and objectives.

4) Implement the recommendations of the financial plan.

5) Review the plan periodically to determine one's progress and make any necessary changes.

Our role in this process, using a team of professional advisers (~~accountants,~~ ~~attorneys~~ ~~ins~~

expertise, we routinely consult and include other professionals, i.e., accountants and attorneys. That is why you will observe these other professions regularly contributing ~~articles~~ ~~in~~ ~~the~~ ~~coming~~ ~~issue~~ ~~of~~

Reprinted with permission of George E. Bates, Bates Financial Services.

STRATEGY

66   **BROADCAST A RADIO COMMERCIAL**

This could be an educational message, comparable to a newspaper advertorial, consisting of tax tips or a timely investment scoop, brought
to the public by you. It could also consist of client testimonials like
those used by planner Mark Negless (Strategy 61), but in an audio format. Choose an appropriate time to air the commercial, such as during
the rush hour (if businesspeople are your target) or during a financially
oriented talk show.

Sometimes buying "fringe time" on radio or television can be even
more productive. Because advertising rates during off-prime-time
hours are significantly cheaper, you'll be able to run your ads more often. Don't overlook cable stations; many offer very inexpensive advertising rates.

Also, if you offer to purchase unused air time over a long enough
period of time, some local, independent or cable stations may give you
a substantial discount, since your commercials will be filling slots they
may not otherwise have been able to sell.

67   SHOULD YOU USE AN AD AGENCY?

Agencies can often make invaluable contributions to your advertising, public relations and overall marketing efforts. Interview a few of them to see what they would suggest for your particular situation. Even if you decide that you'd rather not use one of them, it's likely that their recommendations will give you some food for thought that may translate into ideas you can implement on your own.

If you decide that you want to work with an agency, make sure that you make the account executives or the principals you're working with aware of your budget. Also make sure that the agency has no potential conflicts of interest with any of your competitors.

PUBLIC RELATIONS (P.R.)

68 The Local Media Can Be a Great Source of P.R.

Although we all would like to be quoted in *The Wall Street Journal* or *Money Magazine,* it's far easier, and often more impactful, to get exposure in our own hometowns.

The important thing is to let the media know that you're out there. Ed Gor, with Associates in Financial Planning in Houston, Texas, sends his local newspaper many of the surveys, studies and other newsworthy materials that he receives from the IAFP, along with a cover letter commenting on them. This effort positions him as an expert financial planning resource in the community; whenever the local newspaper seeks information or looks for an opinion on financially oriented matters, he gets called. Any financial professional can provide the same type of service, using materials from his or her applicable trade organization.

⑤ *Newspapers.* Offer to provide a regular column of economic or financial commentary for your local newspaper in addition to providing newsworthy press releases from time to time (see Strategy 69). Write several sample columns and send them to the newspaper's business editor to show that you're available and interested in providing this service. This type of effort will yield several important long-term benefits, the most important of which is name recognition. As your community gets to know you through your column, more people will seek you out for your financial expertise, and your client base will continue to grow. We heard of one financial professional, in fact, who continued to get new clients as a result of his newspaper column for more than two years after he stopped writing it!

Don't neglect the reprint value of these articles too. They can often provide the basis for a small pamphlet or book.

⑤ *Cable stations.* You can also contact your local cable radio or TV station, offering to host a regular weekly financial program, or to appear as a guest speaker on a financially oriented program that already exists. If you're serious about doing a regular series, you might invest in producing a sample show "on spec" with the local station.

You might ask the station to recommend a freelance producer and arrange to rent the station's studio crew for an hour or two for your taping. The topic of your program should be one that has a broad-based market appeal. That way, if your target station decides not to sponsor a regular program for you, you can take your tape to other stations or use it with select clients and prospects.

And if you do obtain the cable station coverage you seek, consider the value of sending a cassette (audio or video) of the program or series to your clients and prospects.

☒ *Previewing your feature.* If you know when an article or TV or radio appearance in which you are participating will run, send an announcement to your clients, prospects and centers of influence so they can look for the upcoming media coverage. This will ensure that your market knows that you're getting good publicity. Even if they miss the actual media appearance, you'll still score points for letting them know about it in advance. Later, when you send them a follow-up copy or recording of the interview or article, it will have greater impact.

69   SUBMIT A PRESS RELEASE

The most common way to get started in a P.R. program is to submit a newsworthy press release to your local newspaper—preferably after obtaining an introduction to the editor. Be aware, however, that editors can receive many press releases each day, so you'll need to make yours stand out. A press release should be short, no more than two to three pages long, double-spaced. Press releases with little or no value include personnel news (like promotions and new hires, for instance), although some local publications will run such items—and if yours do, send them in. Generally, however, effective press releases spark new ideas or shed a different light on old ones.

Include interesting and relevant quotations that can be used as callouts or highlights. Don't hesitate to include photographs, if appropriate, or graphs or charts. All of these elements will make the release more interesting to the editor who receives it and, therefore, more publishable. Begin the press release with a headline, and in the first paragraph identify and summarize the important facts that you wish to communicate—the who, what, when, where and why of the story. Make sure that you send your release to the right person on the editorial staff, not to just anyone.

Even if your press release isn't picked up by the newspaper or journal to which you submit it, you can always use it in your media or marketing kit to show clients and prospects that you keep your finger on the pulse of current financial events and are a source of newsworthy information. In this vein, you can send the release to a variety of other people—to prospects you're trying to turn into clients, for instance, and to directors of organizations at which you're soliciting speaking engagements.

These guidelines will help in preparing and submitting a press release:

- Make sure it's newsworthy.
- Make sure it's accurate.
- Use statistical data to support your story.
- Date it.

- Give it a sharp headline.
- Keep the entire release short and use concise, easy-to-read sentences.
- Include a contact name and telephone number.
- Be aware of closing dates and the lead times necessary for your story to appear in print. For certain magazines, lead times can be as long as three to four months.
- Direct it to the right person.
- Follow up with a phone call (ask if the editor would like any additional information).
- Monitor the results.

For the most part, the daily publications, semiweeklies and biweeklies feature hard news; monthly publications are more oriented toward feature stories and analytical articles. Make sure your news release or article is appropriate to the publication to which you submit it.

"Hard" news stories are those that focus on specific, timely events: "The Dow Jones Industrial Average Plummets 508 Points"; "The Price of Crude Oil Reaches Record High"; or "Fed Reserve Chairman Volcker Steps Down." A "soft" news story would be something like "How the Market Recovered 336 Points Only Three Days after the Crash," explaining, analyzing and commenting on the event. Another type of soft news story might speculatively anticipate the potential repercussions of a future event. Hard news must be published quickly to capture the immediacy of a situation; soft news often provides commentary on the hard news story.

It's unlikely that a financial professional would ever be in a position to supply a publication with hard news. But hard news isn't all that gets printed. Analytical news stories are of great value and interest to the general public, particularly if your news release is timely, well written and expresses an insightful explanation or different point of view. If you act quickly after hard news hits, chances are much better that you'll find yourself in print.

An example of a soft news release is shown in Figure 6–3.

Figure 6-3. "Soft News" Press Release

RELEASE AT WILL   For more information, contact:
                          [Your name and phone number here
                             or the name of a contact at the
                          agency preparing the release for you]

Three Simple Rules Can Protect Against Stock Market Woes

New York City, October 20, 1987. According to financial planner
Jane Jones, an investor can prevent getting caught in a stock market
crash by following several easy but important steps.

The first requires diversifying a portfolio by investment type. By
broadening an investment portfolio to augment stock holdings with
a variety of other investment vehicles, such as bonds, direct real estate investments, and cash or other liquid investments, the investor's
net worth won't be on the line even if the market takes a dive. "Creating a well-balanced portfolio is like following a balanced diet,"
says Jones. "The more variety you include, the healthier you'll be."
Along these lines, she encourages investors to include such assets as
rare coins, gold, stamps, and artwork, among other investments.

For mutual fund assets, Jones advocates using a timing service that
signals the investor as to when to sell and when to buy. Such services analyze broad market trends to provide this valuable information based on extensive research.

Finally, she urges diversification of investment holdings by economic market. Taking advantage of opportunities available in international markets, for example, protects an investor from
becoming dependent on the fortunes of any one economy.

In sum, for Jane Jones and her clientele, protecting a portfolio
from a stock market crash means creating safety valves to prevent
overexposure to risk. These safety valves take the form of a wide
range of investments that keep the portfolio relatively independent
of stock market performance.

# # #

STRATEGY

70 WRITE AN ARTICLE FOR PUBLICATION

Call or send a letter to the appropriate editor of your local paper (i.e., the business or financial editor) and ask if he or she would be interested in receiving and printing an article on some topic that you have in mind. Or just go ahead and write the article and submit it. If it doesn't get published, you can always print it in your own newsletter.

An article for a newspaper or periodical can and should be longer than a news release. It could describe a financial service idea or new investment concept that hasn't received a lot of attention. You'll often find greater acceptance of your submission when your approach is new, different or contrary to common opinion. Your article should say something that no one has said before or at least relay your message in a way that's unusual and that positions you as an expert. Do the research and then carefully consider the audience you want the article to reach, because that audience will determine the tone and content of the piece. Again, include photographs, graphs or charts if they enhance your subject matter.

You can, for example, write an article on an aspect of charitable giving and offer it to one or more charitable organizations for use in their newsletter or for use as a direct mail piece. If possible, your byline should include your address and telephone number so that interested readers (potential clients) wanting to learn more can contact you. Include your telephone number, but prepare yourself for the "blue pencil" of the press, who usually don't like to print more than the name of your firm and its location. Those should be enough, however, for anyone who wants to call to look up the number.

After your article has been published, order reprints of it and send them out to your clients or prospects. In fact, even if the article isn't published, you can still send it out.

s *Articles for trade publications.* You may wish to write a more scholarly article for an industry journal. Trade publications will often be more receptive to your article submissions and will tell you in advance if they're interested. A reprint from an industry journal makes an impressive marketing tool.

71   STAGE AN EVENT FOR PUBLICITY; MAKE IT EASY FOR THE MEDIA

This could be a charitable, fund-raising function that you would sponsor, or an educational symposium. But don't just expect the local media to show up uninvited. Call them and ask them to come; tell them when and where the event is to be held, who's going to be there and what its purpose is. Make it interesting to them.

If you're going to present an educational seminar or symposium, alert your local cable TV supplier as to the date, time and location, as well as to the seminar content. Cable TV producers in some markets often look for financial "filler" material and might be more than willing to videotape your seminar. Afterward you may be able to obtain a copy of the edited tape, which you could use in your marketing efforts. Don't neglect to invite the local press to your seminar as well.

As soon as the event has concluded, prepare a press release and submit it, with photographs if you have them and a transcript of the presentation, to the publications where you'd like the story to appear. Again, if you're not comfortable with your own writing or just don't want to take the time, hire a professional.

72   CREATE A MEDIA KIT

When soliciting an appearance on a radio or television talk show or permission to write an ongoing column or when just preparing press releases, the following items can provide you with an impressive calling card to the media. Each of the items should be typed or printed out on your letterhead, with your name, and firm name, address and telephone number imprinted on it.

- A brief cover letter (two to three paragraphs long) describing who you are, your area of expertise and your availablity to speak; mention the topic you think may be of interest and indicate that you'll follow up with the production staff within a couple of weeks
- A one-page (maximum) description, attached to the cover letter, of why your topic is important to the audience (use short bullet points if possible)
- Article reprints by or about you
- A pre-written, "on-air" introduction, again making it easy for the media
- A sample audiocassette of a seminar or workshop that you've given
- A sample question list that could potentially be used by the program host with you
- A professional photograph (optional)

You'll also find media kits valuable in soliciting speaking engagements from organizations or associations. You should probably develop a slightly different kit for the print media as opposed to the broadcast media as opposed to your other P.R. sources, with suitably tailored letters and inserts for each version.

TO GET STARTED...

1. Choose the *one* idea from this chapter that you liked best.

Strategy: _____

2. How will you implement it? List the steps that you'll need to take.

Implementation Steps:	Date To Complete:	Who Will Implement the Steps If Not You?
1. _____	1. _____	1._____
2. _____	2. _____	2._____
3. _____	3. _____	3._____
4. _____	4. _____	4._____

PART 3

Internal Marketing

7

Delivering the Service and Obtaining Referrals

Internal marketing describes the ongoing service you provide to your clients to help them achieve their financial objectives and to enhance your long-term relationships with them. The time and energy that you put into serving your clients will not only benefit them, but will also be an investment in your own prosperity because well-satisfied clients often generate significant additional business through growth in their accounts as well as through referrals.

Once you've established a portfolio of clients, how do you go about keeping them? Client retention is just as important as getting your prospects in the door. To maximize the number of clients who stick with you, you need to do more than just meet their needs. Providing an extra measure of service or offering your standard service in a novel way will often make the difference in achieving this goal.

Find out what your competition *doesn't like to do* to service your market, and then see if an opportunity exists for you. For instance, if your competitors don't like to get up early, hold breakfast meetings for their clients and offer them to yours. If they think educational materials are a waste, send them to their clients. If they don't offer a particular service, consider providing it. Do what they don't like to do and you'll earn the reputation of being truly different, drawing and keeping the clients that your competitors miss.

Remember, it's tough to make your business grow if you're losing part of your existing client base—particularly if you're losing your best clients. If you don't take a hard look at how to better serve those existing clients, you'll miss out on the easiest way to increase your business.

According to Lawrence A. Krause, well-known advocate of "high-touch" financial planning, clients are lost to financial professionals for the following reasons and in the following proportions:

- One percent die.
- Three percent move away.
- Five percent have friends they prefer to patronize.
- Nine percent are dissatisfied.
- Fourteen percent leave for competitive reasons (i.e., they find a better price or better amenities elsewhere).
- *Sixty-eight percent* are offended by what they perceive as an attitude of indifference or not caring.

Now if, as we assume, you care about your clients, make certain that you let them know it! Demonstrating your interest and your willingness to adjust to your clients' needs can bind them to you forever.

DELIVERING THE SERVICE

Create reasons for your clients to stay with you; make them appreciate how much you're willing to do for them. Typically, the best barometer of business success is how well you meet the goals, needs and expectations of your clients and, ultimately, the financial results that you're able to produce for them over time.

But the financial results that you obtain for your clients aren't enough to build your business. Communication is a critical factor. In fact, sometimes the ability to communicate effectively is the only distinction between otherwise equally well-qualified professionals.

By communicating to your clients and prospects that you take a very personal and special interest in their welfare, you can ultimately leave your competition far behind. As Marshall Field, the pioneer peddler who founded the department store dynasty said, "Goodwill is the one and only asset that the competition cannot undersell or destroy." There are many ways to create goodwill, beginning with your first meeting with a prospect.

REFERRALS FROM CLIENTS

From time to time, you've probably wished that you could clone your best clients. The truth is that you can! Your own clients are your best source of new business because they often will provide you with leads for prospects who are just like them.

A referral from an existing client is the most personal and powerful way of introducing yourself to a prospect. Get your best clients to recommend you to people who might benefit from your services.

REFERRALS FROM OTHER PROFESSIONALS

Networking with other professionals who have various specialties—financial and otherwise—can help you provide better client service and also give you a valuable source of referrals. Cultivate a list of professionals to whom you can refer clients and from whom you will get referrals.

In addition to providing a source of potential referrals, affiliations with other financial professionals will enhance your image. Show your list of professional affiliates to your potential clients, letting them know that these are resources you have available. Ideally, you should try to include two to three individuals within each profession, so that when a client or prospect needs a particular service he or she can have a choice. Additionally, the more individuals you include on the list, the more you'll broaden your opportunity for referrals. Be sure, however, to work only with other financial professionals who meet your service and quality standards and who will reciprocate by sending you referrals. Here are the types of professionals your list could include:

- Financial planners
- Stockbrokers
- Attorneys (a generalist and several types of specialists—tax, estate, corporate, divorce, pension plan, etc.)
- Real estate brokers
- Insurance agents (casualty and life)
- CPAs or accountants (tax and audit)
- Bookkeepers

- Pension plan administrators
- Commercial bankers
- Private bankers
- Trust officers
- Mortgage brokers and correspondents
- Funeral directors

You can find out which financial professionals in your area would be likely candidates for exchanging referrals by sending out a simple questionnaire. The questionnaire would readily enable you to weed out those individuals and firms that would be competing with you—i.e., those promoting the same types of investments, insurance, etc. A key question to include would be "To what outside sources do you refer your clients?" If the answer is "none," you could eliminate that professional from your list.

DELIVERING THE SERVICE

73   SEND YOUR PROSPECTS TO YOUR COMPETITION

Sound crazy? It isn't, really. You see, if you assume that you're going to be a long-term success, you don't *want* clients who "settle" for you because they just aren't aware of other comparable services that are available in the market. Encourage your potential clients to "shop around" and stress how important it is for them to feel comfortable with their choice. You can make it easy for them by actually offering them the names of two or three of your competitors whose work you respect. Your clients will likely be impressed with your sincerity and even more so with the fact that you're not desperate for business. In fact, they may be so impressed that they turn down your offer. In any event, if they ultimately choose to do business with you, they will most likely commit to do so with enthusiasm, confidence and trust. Conversely, if they opt to go with one of your competitors, chances are they made their choice based on feeling more comfortable with that professional. You'll still come out ahead for the following reasons:

1. You've obviously placed the client's good above all other considerations.
2. If the client is truly better off going elsewhere, you've saved yourself from an unproductive relationship.
3. You've given a competitor a valuable referral. Chances are that eventually the competitor will reciprocate in kind because it's human nature to want to return a favor. In fact, you may wish to develop a cadre of professionals, all of whom commit to a specific program of exchanging referrals. That way, on balance, you know you'll get your fair share of potential new clients.
4. The client will remember your good intentions and may in the future present you with some business opportunities—if not directly, then through a referral or perhaps several referrals.

5. The approach is so refreshingly out of the ordinary that the prospect will probably turn into your client.

Remember, in the long run, you don't need or even want every potential client who knocks at your door. You only need the ones who are right for you.

74   LET YOUR CLIENTS KNOW HOW IMPORTANT THEY ARE

It's important for you to contribute as much as possible to your clients' comfort. On a physical level, you can create a warm and friendly environment in your office through your choice of furniture and decor; on an emotional level, you can be an empathetic, active listener.

⑤ *Welcoming them.* Actively welcome them when they come to your office. A bulletin board is one way to do this. When you're expecting a particular married couple, for instance, you can place a big "Welcome, Mr. and Mrs. Jones" on the board.

⑤ *Refreshments.* Recognizing that the early mornings and late afternoons are times when some clients lack energy, Carol A. Wright, a San Francisco-based financial planner, provides muffins, fruit, cheese and beverages for her client meetings that are held during those times. Not only do the snacks give them energy, but nibbling on food constitutes a familiar and relaxing activity that often increases the clients' receptivity to her ideas.

⑤ *A rolling office.* One financial professional suggests an ambulatory office. He carries most of his supplies in his van and visits clients in their own environments where they feel more at ease and in control.

⑤ *Flexibility with fees.* You may find it appropriate to give your clients a fee option. For example, financial planners can receive payment in any of the following ways:

- Fee only
- Fee, offset by commissions
- Fee and commissions
- Commissions only

Many financial professionals have a number of payment structures from which to choose. You might consider giving your clients a payment option to show your flexibility and willingness to work with them in a way that will accommodate their needs as well as yours. If you pick a single payment approach, do make sure that it fits the market segment you target. For example, tier II isn't as fee-oriented as tiers III and IV, so commissions would be the more appropriate payment structure here. Be aware, however, that if you provide too many options, you may have to spend more time than you'd like addressing your clients' potential confusion.

S *Reminder cards.* Send your clients a reminder card for appointments, and include a map with directions on how to get to your office. Confirm the appointment with them the day before or the morning of the meeting. The result: very few missed appointments.

S *Fax machines.* With their permission, use telefaxes for your top clients. Don't hesitate to fax them timely information, rather than sending it through the mail. It will build their confidence in your services, showing them that you keep your finger on the pulse of vital information, filtering news of important events and investment opportunities through to them.

S *A WATS line.* For those professionals who serve a market area that includes more than one telephone area code, consider offering an incoming WATS line to save them the cost of a call to your office.

S *The "$1 million question."* At the end of the first interview, and after every subsequent meeting, ask your clients this powerful question: *"Is there anything else I can help you with, or do you have any questions or concerns, that we haven't covered, which I can address?"* Your clients will feel good about your investment recommendations when they realize that you take a genuine interest in helping them and in spending whatever time is necessary to do so. And, importantly, they will often share an insight, an insecurity or an idea that will give you a valuable key to aiding them further. This $1 million question ensures that your own presentation doesn't prevent you from hearing your clients' concerns. (As a general hint, if they are somewhat hesitant or unresponsive, it often helps to be very specific, asking about particular issues in which they may want help or clarification.)

75 Make Sure Your Clients Know the Full Range of Your Services

Too often, clients just aren't familiar with all of the services you offer and what their responsibilities and obligations are within your business relationship. The solution is simple: Provide them with a list of all the services you offer and the types of products you sell so that they know to call you rather than someone else when the need arises.

One way that you can do this is to create a catalog or brochure of benefits so that clients and prospects know exactly what you have to offer. The catalog would list all the basic services you provide, and perhaps the following extras:

- Phone calls and conferences as needed
- Periodic newsletter
- Annual client appreciation dinner or event
- Check-cashing service for clients
- Special office use for out-of-town clients

[s] *Showing your clients and prospects your work.* When a potential client comes in to see you, wouldn't you like to be able to show that prospect exactly what you do? It's easy. All you have to do is create several "case studies" to illustrate the types of services you provide. For example, if you're a stockbroker you probably have quite a few stories about clients who came in with portfolios that weren't performing in accordance with their expectations. Based on your recommendations and active modifications, the portfolios turned around and became profitable. Your case study would describe a particular client's circumstances and what happened based on your intervention over a period of time. If the client agreed, you could even make his or her name available for reference upon request.

It's a good idea to develop several of these types of case studies to include in your image kit and for use with potential clients. They bring life and color to what you do, clearly relating your services to your prospects' own needs.

Each study should be concise—no more than one typewritten page, if possible. It should follow a three-part format, succinctly describing what the client's circumstances were, how you addressed them, and the results you obtained.

Case studies have another use as well. You can incorporate them into a direct mail campaign to court potential prospects. Mail a series of case studies—professionally written, designed and printed—to your target market in a sequence of "drips." The studies would amplify a variety of approaches to different problems that affect your target market. Similarly, you can use this series for advertorials in local print publications, or even for radio advertising. They will reinforce that you're focused on your market and can deliver creative solutions to its specific needs.

For your own legal protection, ask your firm's compliance officer or your personal attorney to clear your case study for marketing use. You may need to incorporate a disclaimer acknowledging that past performance doesn't necessarily predict future results.

[s] *Agendas and checklists.* After the first meeting with a client, prepare an agenda detailing the purpose of the service that you're proposing, reviewing the client's objectives, and outlining possible strategies for implementation. Provide a checklist to your client; for each step in the planning process, it should identify whether the client or you will take action, and by what date.

You can produce a preprinted form for use with all your clients or create a form on your computer that you can customize and print out on the spot to accommodate your clients' individual needs and circumstances. An example of the type of form a financial planner might develop is seen in Figure 7–1.

[s] *Giveaways.* Give your clients something to remember you by. A document locator, for instance, is an extremely useful personal reference tool and one that will always remind the client of you since it will be imprinted with your name, address and telephone number. The form identifies the location of important financial data such as wills; insurance policies; deeds of ownership; birth, marriage and death certificates; and safe-deposit boxes. If you mail it to your clients and prospects, stress that it's free.

Figure 7-1. Strategic Planning Checklist

		Responsibility	
		Client	Planner
1.	Bring in will.	x	
2.	Take inventory of safe-deposit box.	x	
3.	Summarize stock portfolio yields.		x
4.	Call tax attorney to introduce planner.	x	
5.	Get copy of prior year's tax return.	x	
6.	Arrange meeting between client's attorney and accountant.		x

STRATEGY
76   STAY IN CLOSE TOUCH WITH YOUR CLIENTS AND PROSPECTS

Some professionals think you should be in touch at least once a month. In any case, it's important not to let too much time go by without some contact. The important thing is to keep your name in your clients' minds. Remember the Drip Method (Strategy 40). Call your clients periodically to see if they have any questions or if there's anything you can help them with. What a refreshing change it will be for them—instead of hearing the sales pitch they may have come to expect.

Keep your clients up to date. Help them stay abreast of economic and business trends; make sure they know that you're keeping your finger on the industry pulse and that you're there as an informational and educational resource for them.

[S] *Contacting your clients when you have news.* It has been said that "people don't care how much you know until they know how much you care." If there's good news about an investment, your clients should be the first to know. They should also be the first to know if there's bad news, or even if the possibility of bad news exists. You should have a computerized investment data base that can quickly give you the names of all your clients who are in any one particular investment. If the situation, whatever it is, gets resolved and the unpleasant event doesn't come to pass, you'll have reinforced your clients' trust by confronting them directly and honestly. Even if it does come to pass, you will have alerted them appropriately, and they will respect you for it.

Call your top clients and send a letter to all the rest to share ideas or new product information that you've picked up at the seminars and workshops you've attended. This is an opportune time to contact your clients and a great way to generate some excitement.

Send them newspaper and magazine clippings that may interest them or be relevant to their particular circumstances. Send them your own article reprints and audiocassettes too. Let your clients know that you have their best financial interests in mind.

[s] *Calling your clients for no reason at all.* You don't always need to have something important to say to your clients in order to call. Don't hesitate to call them just to say hello and let them know that you're thinking about them. It might be that on your way to work you happen to pass by a baseball field where a little league team is at practice, and it makes you think about a client's son, Jaime, who plays on a little league team. Pick up the phone and call the client! Ask how Jaime is doing. Showing this type of personal interest and attention will almost always enhance your relationship with your client, bringing the client closer to you.

[s] *Remembering their birthdays.* You may consider including with their birthday greeting a succinct and well-designed questionnaire asking them if they are aware of all of the services you provide (and then listing them); the questionnaire should provide space for them to reply and indicate which particular service or product they'd like more information on. You can send a birthday greeting to each member of a client's immediate family too.

[s] *Celebrating anniversaries.* The date when your client signed on with you was an important day for both you and the client! Let your clients know how much they mean to you by sending them a card or a gift to celebrate their anniversary of doing business with you.

[s] *Avoiding "telephone tag."* When a client calls and you're away from the office or unavailable to take the call for some other reason, have your assistant ask when an appropriate time would be for you to return the call. This simple gesture will clearly communicate your attentiveness and commitment to deliver premium client service. Also, your fax machine can come in handy if you keep missing each other.

77   DO YOUR CLIENTS A FAVOR

You can provide exceptional, out-of-the-ordinary service to your clients by giving them bonus extras.

S *Sharing your discoveries.* Stuart M. Purcell of Purcell Wealth Management in San Rafael, California, a CPA and financial counselor, offers his clients a unique ongoing service. The core of his marketing plan is providing a professional service that adds value to his clients' lives. Taking the attitude that if he does someone a special favor, it "makes that person's day," he developed the idea of letting his clients know about the services, shops and other retail establishments that he finds offer exceptional value and customer attention. He does this through a graphically illustrated flier, "When I Find Someone Who Provides Exemplary Personal Service, I Tell My Friends..." (Figure 7-2), which he gives to clients and prospects. According to Purcell, this simple yet very effective service has saved his clientele thousands of dollars (in paying "wholesale" versus "retail" prices), and the retailers he recommends benefit from the added business, too. This can be used as a direct mail promotion as well.

S *Sending your clients to the extra-service bank.* Often you'll find that small or private banks are eager to get your clients as new customers. Consider working out a deal with the bank. You can offer to refer your clients if the bank will give them a special service. Such service might, for example, include a bonus yield on a certificate of deposit for a specific period, a free checking account or a free safe-deposit box. Your clients will benefit from the service; you'll score points for giving them a valuable referral; and the bank will acquire new customers. Everyone wins. You might also be able to structure an arrangement in which, after you refer a designated number of new clients, the bank sponsors a seminar for you.

S *Newsletters.* Newsletters serve as an excellent marketing tool and also provide a great way to stay in touch with your clients simply by

Figure 7–2. "I Tell My Friends" Promotion

Purcell
Wealth
Management

When I find someone who provides *exemplary personal service,*

I TELL MY FRIENDS . . .

By: Stuart M. Purcell
November 1989

Gold Key Sales & Leasing

Auto/Equipment Purchasing and Financing

Michael A. Dunmore
560 Hartz Avenue, Suite 204
Danville, CA 94526

(415) 743-0231
(415) 246-9317 (Pager)
(415) 743-0451 (FAX)

Steve McElroy

<u>Complete</u> Automobile Detailing
(at your home or office - $50)

(415) 897-6081

John's Shoe Repair

975 Grand Avenue
San Rafael, CA 94901
(between 3rd and 4th)

(415) 456-9922

(415) 485-6814
1811 Grand Ave., Suite B
San Rafael, California 94901

PROMO
SERVICE.PWM

*Securities Offered Through a Registered Representative &
Integrated Resources Equity Corp., Member NASD & SIPC*

Reprinted with permission by Stuart M. Purcell, Purcell Wealth Management (San Rafael, CA).

keeping them up to date (see Strategy 60). If you don't want to produce a newsletter, just send out a simple, informative letter. In word-processed form letters to clients, always include a personal line or two that you can change from letter to letter; it provides a nice touch to particularly address each individual client.

You can include with your letter, on a monthly or quarterly basis, a one-page summary of recommended products, showing samples of each type—oil, gas, real estate, equipment leasing and mutual funds, for example. You can then follow up to see if any of your clients would like a prospectus. You should have your attorney review this type of material, however, to ensure that you don't violate any technical securities laws by the omission of necessary disclaimer language.

Alternatively, you might consider a two-part newsletter. Part one would contain general information and commentary—more suitable for prospects and sources of P.R.; part two would be more product-specific, having a narrower appeal to your existing clientele.

78   HAVE AN ANNUAL MEETING AND/OR PUBLISH AN ANNUAL REPORT

Even if you're a sole proprietor, or if your organization consists of just a few financial professionals, you should strive to offer your clientele a broad enough range of services and benefits to allow you to compete with a large organization.

An annual meeting provides a good opportunity to get together and recap the events of the past year, to share your observations on general economic and political trends, and to let your clients know what's new with your business and what your plans and goals are for the coming year. Many professionals call such an annual meeting "Client Appreciation Night."

After the meeting, you can print your annual report or produce it in audiocassette form, or do both, and send it to those clients who weren't able to attend the meeting.

79   WHAT ABOUT SENDING GIFTS?

For an appropriate occasion, a gift can be a thoughtful gesture that will garner a lot of goodwill. To enhance your own professional image, the gift should generally be one that's related to your clients' financial or business affairs. Of course, gifts that don't have a specific business purpose tend to make a more personal impression, so they too can be worthwhile.

You can give your clients gifts for several different reasons:

- Holidays
- When you get a referral
- Upon the client's reaching an investment milestone; a stockbroker, for example, accomplishing a number of especially large or significant trades for a client, might consider sending the client a gift

Whatever the gift type, gifts are often most effective when they are least expected. Don't hesitate to create your own unique occasions for gift-giving.

⑤ *One-dollar bills.*   For the New Year, consider sending your clients a gift to inaugurate the new year. For example, every year, Texas-based planner Lee Pennington sends his clients (and many potential clients) a dollar bill, enclosed in a special gift envelope that bears the inscription "Here's your first dollar of investment profit for the year." This powerful idea gets attention.

⑤ *Thanksgiving gifts.*   How many people expect to receive a gift on Thanksgiving? Yet this holiday represents a perfect opportunity to express your thanks for your clients' business. Giving a Thanksgiving gift is a way to make you truly different. Moreover, the impact of a gift given at an unexpected time like Thanksgiving won't be diluted by other gifts as it would, for instance, if it were given at Christmas.

⑤ *Gift certificates.*   Another planner mails a gift certificate to each of his best clients for them to give to a friend or associate who might benefit from financial planning services. The certificates offer a free consultation for 30-45 minutes on any financial topic, and they make excellent Christmas gifts from the clients to their friends. It's a nice touch that also happens to provide a great source of referrals. How about getting your referral partners to give you free gift certificates?

⬜ *Acknowledging them with a gift that keeps on giving.* Giving gifts when your clients, or prospects, least expect them can be a very effective way of "dripping" on those individuals. You can send your good clients a gift that gets repeated every month or every few months over a period of time. For example, the most obvious example of this type of gift would be a "fruit of the month" basket. To the client, the first basket will obviously reflect your business association. The second basket, however, will come as a surprise. And subsequent fruit gifts will truly amaze and impress the client because they arrive for no reason other than your generous goodwill.

⬜ *Other professionals meeting your gift-giving needs.* Toward the end of the year, consider contacting one of the major accounting firms in your area to get a quantity of their printed booklets on tax tips. The accounting firms will appreciate the exposure, and you'll be able to obtain a high-value client giveaway that won't cost you much.

Here are some other gift ideas for your clients:

- Books on investments, tax or estate planning or any topics that you know hold a special interest for your clients
- Subscriptions to a financial journal or business publication
- Tickets to a presentation or seminar on an economic or investment-oriented topic
- A luncheon or dinner invitation to a private club that features interesting speakers
- An educational videocassette or audiocassette
- Specially imprinted file folders or binders that will help organize personal or business documents
- A calculator with special features (such as calculating bond yields, amortization schedules or internal rates of return)

- A financial software package that you like (although this may be prohibitively expensive to give to everyone, you may find it appropriate for your best clients)
- Commerce Clearing House booklets on tax laws or Social Security benefits
- Business organizers, such as Day-Timers™ and expense logs

80   PROVIDE ADDITIONAL FINANCIAL AND BUSINESS SERVICES

Make yours a true renaissance practice by incorporating new services that your competition may not offer. You can develop the skills and expertise to provide many of these services yourself, or you can team up with other financial professionals. The bottom line is that by offering a wide range of different services, you'll be able to provide a one-stop shop to take care of all of your clients' financial needs.

S *Bookkeeping and tax preparation.* Why should your clients go elsewhere to obtain these essential services? You may even find that they become one of the most lucrative components of your business.

Some financial professionals claim that offering tax preparation services tends to improve the quality of their ongoing service since all areas of investment have important tax implications. Although tax preparation requires a significant time commitment, it's easier now than ever before to acquire the skills and expertise to prepare tax returns due to the availability of new software programs that simplify the process and make it more accurate. Be aware, however, that in order to be able to represent taxpayers before the Internal Revenue Service and the U.S. Tax Court, you must become an "enrolled agent," a designation awarded by the IRS based on passing a comprehensive examination on the U.S. Tax Code. You should check with your attorney or your firm's legal counsel to help identify your responsibilities in providing this service.

S *Legal documentation.* Help your clients with their wills, living trusts, prenuptial agreements, divorce settlements and other legal issues. In order to do this, you will, of course, need to enlist (either by hiring or association) the services of a qualified legal expert.

S *Life, disability, medical and business insurance.* Everyone needs these services. By providing them, you create yet another level of value for your clients.

[s] *Your expertise in negotiations.* You can provide a valuable, often overlooked, service to your clients by assisting in the process of real estate purchases, procuring financing, consummating other large purchases, and acting as an impartial intermediary in financial transactions involving your clients and their friends, relatives or close associates.

[s] *Asset management capabilities.* Assets under management can provide one of the most lucrative means of building your business because as your clients' asset portfolios grow, so will your income. You can work with a professional asset manager to do this. The beauty of assets under management is that even when times are slow and you're not actively working with a lot of clients, you will still have a constant source of income and one that can grow disproportionately to the amount of time you actually spend servicing those accounts.

Offer a wide range of services to your clients so that even when the economy is sluggish, you'll still be able to provide services that your clients will need. Make yourself as indispensable as you can, but make sure that you're set up to deliver first-rate results for whatever additional services you promote.

OBTAINING REFERRALS

STRATEGY

81 Don't Hesitate To Ask Your Clients for Referrals

You can ask for referrals from your clients as part of the "payment" for your services. Don't be shy. This is an excellent way to get referrals. Raymond E. Moore of Chubb Securities in Richmond, Virginia, bills for referrals. He sends an actual "statement" to his clients after he has completed his work for them, requesting three different referrals as payment, a clever way to remind his clients of their prior commitments to him.

If you adopt this method, however, don't be indiscriminate. Ask for referrals only from your best clients. Here are a few other ways to ask for them.

[S] *Hitting a home run.* "Mr. or Ms. Client," you would ask, "how can I hit a home run for you? What would it take for you to be so delighted with my service that you would not only give me some referrals but without my asking you, you would call your friends, relatives or business associates to tell them what a terrific job I've been doing? What would I have to do for you to do that?"

Asking this type of question has several benefits. First, it will give you an understanding of what is most important to that client and enable you to do a better job for the client over the long term. Second, it will enhance the client's comfort level in doing business with you, since you'll be showing how much you care about meeting the client's particular needs. And finally, if you've listened well to the response you receive, you'll be sure to get the referrals you want.

[S] *The "Tupperware™ approach."* See if your existing clients would be interested in sponsoring an afternoon tea or coffee hour for their friends or associates, during which you would talk about a financially oriented topic, such as tax or estate planning, investments for the self-employed or developing a will. It's a great way to gain exposure to potential clients and to generate additional strong referrals.

[S] *Referrals up front.* Try asking for referrals after your initial fact-finding interview, rather than waiting until later on. If you do a good job during the interview, your clients will be impressed at the thoroughness of your work and will feel inclined to refer others to you.

[S] *Selecting a prime moment.* You can ask for referrals after a client makes an investment decision. This provides a perfect moment for you to ask the client if he or she knows anyone else who might benefit from such an investment opportunity.

[S] *Asking the right questions.* Focus your clients' attention on the type of referral you'd like to get. If you just ask for referrals, your clients may not know how to respond or whom to recommend. For example, you should ask your clients questions that identify your target market(s), such as "Do you know anyone who

- is relocating to this area?"
- has recently sold a business or plans to sell one?"
- has recently retired?"
- is having a tax problem?"
- is planning to retire?"
- is in the process of a divorce?"
- is about to get married?"
- has infant children?"
- is as successful as you are?"
- has needs similar to yours?"

Alternatively, you can ask a client the following general question: "If you were a [stockbroker, financial planner, accountant etc.], whom would you want to help first among your acquaintances or business colleagues?" Then ask if the client would call that individual and arrange an appointment for you.

Another approach might be to ask your clients who are in business for the names of their biggest competitors (who are often their friends). Asking for this type of referral, of course, assumes that you provide personal financial planning services and that no conflict of interest would arise from developing a business relationship with one of your client's competition.

⒮ *Confiding in your client.* Identify a list of prospects who are in the same profession or who have similar interests as one of your particularly good clients. Show it to your client and explain that you plan to call on these people and ask if the client knows them and if he or she could perhaps provide an introduction. The client will usually be able to spot a few friends. One financial planner we know takes this technique a step further, after getting the list of referrals, by asking her clients if they would feel comfortable providing any information about the prospect that might be helpful to her. When the planner calls on a prospect that one of her clients has told her something about, she has a more personal way of introducing herself and is that much closer to getting an appointment.

⒮ *Referrals by mail.* A Canadian financial planner we heard about asks his clients the following question before he sends them any information: "May I put an extra copy into your envelope for an associate? I'd very much like to have clients with interests similar to yours." Include a note with the extra information, which says something like, "For a friend or associate who might find this helpful."

⒮ *An evening of entertainment.* This could, for instance, be a sports event. Ask the client to invite a friend or associate, or you can invite a designated prospect yourself. Your client will likely endorse your services.

⒮ *Inviting clients' guests to a seminar.* At the seminar, acknowledge that many of the attendees are there because their friends invited them or asked that they be invited. Thank everyone for coming; be warm, positive, appreciative and encouraging.

⒮ *Keeping several referral letters on file.* Ask your satisfied clients to write a letter of referral for you. If they don't have the time or if it's difficult for them to write their own original letter, you can give them several suggested letters that you've written yourself, which they can then simply sign. You should provide the postage and have the signed letter returned to you so that you can control the timing of its mailing.

[S] *Returning their favors.* Ask your clients for copies of *their* brochures and cards for you to give away when appropriate. Just as you would like referrals from them, you may also like to refer your other associates and clients to them.

Be sure to thank your clients for the referrals they give you. Always follow up with a referring client by sending a thank-you note or some other type of acknowledgment to let the client know how much you appreciate the referral(s). Jack Prior, of Prior Financial Planning in San Diego, California, sends his referring clients a one-troy-ounce silver coin after the client who's been referred purchases an investment or insurance product.

You can even offer your clients special thank-you gifts to get them to generate referrals. John A. Kiriaze with Financial Advisors in La Jolla, California, and his wife—both of whom are FAA-licensed hot-air balloon pilots—take their best clients and those who generate the most referrals on complimentary hot-air balloon rides.

Another general way to thank your clients and remind them how much you value referrals is by placing a short blurb at the bottom of your newsletter that says something like: "For those of you who have referred your friends, family and associates to me, once again, thank you. Referrals are the most personal and professionally satisfying way for my business to grow."

82   Make Sure That Your Name and Phone Number Are Accessible

One way to accomplish this is to give your clients, prospects and centers of influence some useful printed material in card form that they can carry around with them in their purses or wallets. It could, for instance, be a small calendar; a metric conversion chart; or a card imprinted with tax tips, important financial dates of the year or even area codes of major metropolitan and business areas—any of which items would also be imprinted with your name, address and telephone number. That way, everyone would have easy reference to your name and number and would be able to pass them along to friends, associates or relatives when appropriate. In fact, for that reason, you should send or give them two. You can also use a printed "giveaway" like this to further your general marketing efforts.

s *Planting your business cards to see if they bear fruit.* For those financial professionals just starting out, try planting your business card in key tax, investment and financial planning books at the local library. We're told it works.

Don't be hesitant about giving them away. Give two business cards to everyone you meet so they in turn can give one of them away. The prospect may not have an immediate need for your services, but may very well know or encounter someone who does.

83   DO SOMETHING SO SPECIAL FOR YOUR CLIENTS THAT THEY TELL EVERYONE ABOUT IT

This idea comes from Charles H. Kuhtz III of Stifel, Nicolaus & Company in Milwaukee, Wisconsin, and it's a gem. He recommends that, for elderly clients who may have a difficult time getting to your office because of poor eyesight or arthritis, or for those who are reluctant to come for other reasons, you offer to buy lunch at a to-go eating establishment (Kentucky Fried Chicken, for example) and take it to their home for your meeting. They'll tell everyone!

STRATEGY
84 CREATE NETWORKING OPPORTUNITIES

Networking opportunities don't often occur by themselves; you have to carefully plan them.

[S] *Your clients' other advisers.* Every time you get a new client, consider calling that client's attorney or accountant or financial planner to say that you have a client in common. It will establish immediate rapport, which might develop into a relationship that could yield mutual client referrals.

[S] *Hosting a networking party.* Glenda Kemple, a Certified Financial Planner and CPA with Quest Capital Management in Dallas, Texas, creates special "networking receptions" for Quest Capital's centers of influence. She asks her clients for the names of the attorneys and CPAs they work with and then holds a reception exclusively for them. They are given a tour of Quest Capital's offices and have the opportunity to exchange business cards with everyone in attendance and talk about what they do. Refreshments typically include cheese, wine and fruit. Although Kemple points out that it usually takes more than one contact with other professionals to establish a relationship in which referrals can be exchanged, the receptions set the stage for renewed contact. These receptions have proven so valuable to Quest Capital that the company hosts them as frequently as once a month.

[S] *Inviting other financial professionals and their clients to your seminars.* When you sponsor a seminar for the public, give ten free tickets to an accountant or attorney or stockbroker to give to his or her best clients.

[S] *Attending the meetings and seminars of other professionals.* You might consider joining an association for CPAs, for example, or for attorneys or mortgage brokers. When a meeting or seminar is going to be held, find out who will be there and plan to attend. Getting there early will enable you to talk to the speaker, as well as to have more time to pick and choose the people you want to meet. Develop some good questions and answers ahead of time, so that you don't have to waste time on unproductive "small talk."

85 SOMEONE'S CASTOFFS MAY BECOME YOUR GOOD CLIENTS

An insurance specialist we heard from tells other agents he knows to give him their rejects—the clients they can't help or, for any number of reasons, want to eliminate from their client list. He finds that the referrals he gets this way often turn into very good clients.

Also, as mentioned in Strategy 73, you can refer your own prospects to your competition so they can shop and compare the services that you have to offer. You'll probably find that if you begin to do this, you'll receive referrals from your competition as well.

86   HELP OTHER PROFESSIONALS PROVIDE BETTER SERVICE

Especially during real estate booms, but even in difficult markets, many people have substantial equity in their homes that could be more productively employed if freed up through a second or additional mortgage. With interest still fully deductible for most people, the use of leverage, combined with smart investing, can help them reach financial independence faster. So, consider cooperating with mortgage brokers. They can refer you to clients of theirs who might benefit from your investment expertise. Obviously, however, any borrowing against home equity should be prudent and consistent with the objectives and risk tolerance of each particular investor.

James J. Hughes of Hughes Financial Management in Newburyport, Massachussetts, works closely with a large casualty insurance agency. The insurance company benefits by having the ability to offer personal financial planning services to its clients, and Hughes' firm is kept so busy that it has little need to prospect for new business.

Similarly, Tom Dillon, with Bruno Stolze & Company in St. Louis, Missouri, has an arrangement with a discount stock brokerage firm that provides him with an ongoing stream of new clients. Often, an investor will seek investment planning advice that goes beyond the scope of the stock brokerage firm; in those cases, the investor gets referred to the financial planner. Similarly, from time to time, an estate tax attorney needs a broker to help liquidate a client's portfolio; and a financial planner may need the expertise of an insurance agent.

You can also get to know firms specializing in relocation services. Find out which firms—REALTORS® and others—specialize in providing relocation services to executives and managers of major employers in your area. Get in touch with the relocation service and offer to provide your brochure for inclusion in the packets of information sent to relocating executives. Having you involved in the process will benefit not only the individuals and families who are relocating, but the relocation service as well. The relocation firm will appreciate your financial expertise and will come to rely on you for prequalifying buyers, a task it would otherwise have to perform itself. The relocating executive will appreciate your assistance in determining how much to spend and perhaps even how to obtain and structure the best financing available and will call on you for your expertise in other affairs when he or she eventually moves into the area.

[S] *Certificates for free service.* Michael K. Stein of Financial Planning & Management in Boulder, Colorado, suggests the following technique, which has worked exceptionally well for his firm. The specific application is to solicit client referrals from real estate agents.

"Real estate agents are not in a position to give specific advice to a potential buyer about the amount they should spend for a new home, the monthly payments they should undertake or the amount that should be paid as a down payment," he points out. "A financial planner, however, is in a position to do that. As a means of setting up the real estate sale, we have found that some real estate agents are willing to pay us a nominal and fixed fee for working with a potential buyer to formulate specific recommendations.

"Our technique involves the use of engraved certificates, which we buy in quantities of 1,000 at about five cents per certificate. We then use desktop publishing and a copy machine to produce small quantities of certificates to use for specific marketing tasks."

Stein stresses that the use of the certificate (shown in Figure 7–3) revolves around four key points:

1. "The certificate has the look and feel of money, and we take pains to present it in a way that enhances the sense of value."
2. "It obligates us to do something specific, either as a complimentary service or for a fee."
3. "We have the certificates distributed by third parties as a benefit offered by that third party."
4. "We acknowledge the distribution of a certificate by sending some expression of gratitude to the person who gave it to the client/ buyer."

The real estate agent presents the certificate to the potential buyer as a service. When his analysis is complete, Stein gives a copy to the real estate agent (with the client's prior written approval) so that the real estate agent can then zero in on appropriate properties.

Figure 7-3.   Certificate for Free Service

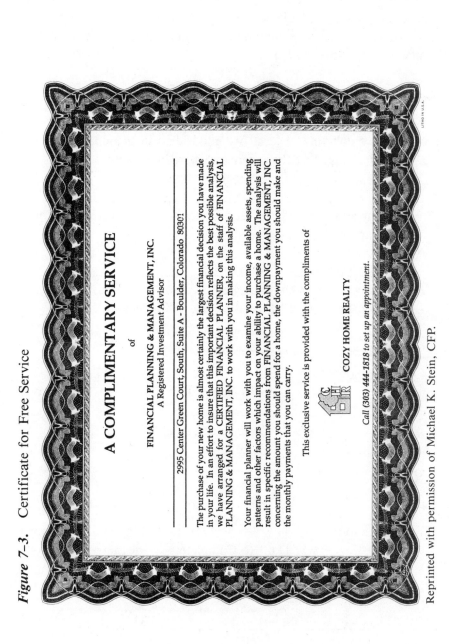

A COMPLIMENTARY SERVICE

of

FINANCIAL PLANNING & MANAGEMENT, INC.
A Registered Investment Advisor

2995 Center Green Court, South, Suite A - Boulder, Colorado 90301

The purchase of your new home is almost certainly the largest financial decision you have made in your life. In an effort to insure that this important decision reflects the best possible analysis, we have arranged for a CERTIFIED FINANCIAL PLANNER, on the staff of FINANCIAL PLANNING & MANAGEMENT, INC. to work with you in making this analysis.

Your financial planner will work with you to examine your income, available assets, spending patterns and other factors which impact on your ability to purchase a home. The analysis will result in specific recommendations from FINANCIAL PLANNING & MANAGEMENT, INC. concerning the amount you should spend for a home, the downpayment you should make and the monthly payments that you can carry.

This exclusive service is provided with the compliments of

COZY HOME REALTY

Call (303) 444-1818 to set up an appointment.

Reprinted with permission of Michael K. Stein, CFP.

As Stein aptly describes it, "Win, win, win. Everyone benefits. The client/buyer gets good advice at no cost. The real estate agent gets the sale. We get a great introduction to a potential client who is frequently a newcomer to the community."

TO GET STARTED...

1. If you didn't find at least five good ideas in this chapter, something's wrong. List them here and start implementing: _____
   _____
   _____

2. List any additional ideas that occurred to you as you were reading the chapter: _____
   _____
   _____

3. Choose any two of the strategies listed above that you'd like to try. Identify the steps you'll need to take to implement them.

Strategy: _____

Implementation Steps:	Date To Complete:	Who Will Implement the Steps If Not You?
1._____	1._____	1._____
2._____	2._____	2._____
3._____	3._____	3._____
4._____	4._____	4._____

Strategy: _____

Implementation Steps:	Date To Complete:	Who Will Implement the Steps If Not You?
1._____	1._____	1._____
2._____	2._____	2._____
3._____	3._____	3._____
4._____	4._____	4._____

8 *Sustaining Your Success*

A wise man once said, "When you start coasting, there's only one way to go, and that's downhill."

Complacency can destroy the greatest measure of success. When business is thriving, it's easy to believe that the momentum will independently continue forever. When you're busy with client service, many activities (like marketing) tend to fall by the wayside, and yet this is often the time when they're needed the most.

In the dynamic financial services business, it's important to work against becoming one's own impediment to success. The way to do this is to commit to a program of flexibility and growth, to be willing to change in an ever-changing world. A true renaissance professional maintains a competitive edge by continually looking inward with an eye to improve.

EVALUATING YOUR SERVICES

How well are you doing? You have two basic indicators of the quality of service you provide. One is client retention; the longer they stay, the more satisfied they are. The second is the growth in dollar volume that you achieve; a growing volume indicates that you're acquiring new clients who will enhance your business.

Analyzing your own operation should become an important and regular part of your business activities. You should develop a method of assessing the caliber of services you provide so that you can improve the areas in which you may be weak and expand on the areas in which you're already successful. Try to establish a set schedule for doing this—once each quarter may be appropriate—to gain an objective view of your value to your target market.

RUNNING A LEAN OPERATION

It really pays to keep your own operating costs low and run an efficient operation. This doesn't mean that you have to be cheap; you just need to avoid spending money excessively on your own office operations. For instance, consider whether you really need *all* of those subscriptions and association memberships that you may have. Cancelling some of them will not only save money (which could then perhaps be spent on marketing), but it will also free up some of your time for working with prospective and existing clients.

Be careful too not to spend all of your success. Put a substantial portion of your profits back into your business to leverage your time and productivity: Consider buying that additional computer or laser printer you need, and consider hiring another assistant, rather than splurging on a new boat or a sports car. Building a business means investing in it.

FOLLOWING THE 80/20 RULE

Chances are that your revenues are generated according to one of the most famous truisms of business: About 80 percent of your business comes from approximately 20 percent of your clients. That 20 percent probably deserves special, if not extraordinary, treatment. You probably don't devote 80 percent of your time to those clients, but consider that if you focused more of your energy on them, you'd probably be able to enhance the productivity of their accounts. And if those 20 percent created only 10 percent more business, your overall volume would grow by 8 percent.

Make sure that all of your staff know who the 20 percent are and that they merit special attention. Identify too those clients who have the potential to generate business that's on a par with your top 20 percent. Be sure to update your 80/20 lists regularly and post them somewhere in your office so that all of your staff can see who they are. Clients' circumstances change, and you may find that some of your 80-percent clients migrate into the top 20 percent and vice versa.

PROFESSIONAL DEVELOPMENT

There's no such thing as too much self-improvement. Because we live in an environment of constant change—in technology as well as the economy—we need to continually improve ourselves to keep up with new product developments and to ensure that we don't lag behind our competition. An undertaking in self-improvement may cost some time as well as money, but it will in essence be an investment in yourself, and one that will pay off royally.

MANAGING YOUR TIME

Consider this: If you save 10 percent of your time, it will be like giving yourself a 10-percent raise without any extra effort. We all tend to fall into habits that, unquestioned, become permanent time-wasters. Your staff can help save you time if you let them. All you need do is learn how to delegate responsibility to let them assume more of your work load. Your time is best spent working directly with your clients and prospects; your staff should do almost everything else.

Consider taking a time management course every three or four years; you'll find it a productive investment in your own professional development.

87   Call Your Office in the Guise of a Client

Test the response you get when you call your office as a potential or existing client looking for assistance. If you don't feel comfortable doing this yourself (perhaps one of your staff will recognize your voice), you can ask someone else to do it for you while you listen in to the conversation on another extension.

S *Good answering systems.* You know how frustrating it can be to be placed on "hold" indefinitely while the operator/receptionist answers other calls or attends to other obligations. It has probably happened to you far too often. Don't make your own clients wait before they get a response—even if that response is that you're not available to take their call and will have to return it later.

88 ASK YOUR CLIENTS TO EVALUATE YOUR SERVICES

This may be the best way to find out how you're doing, since it involves going directly to the horse's mouth. You can approach your clients for feedback in a variety of ways.

[s] *Client councils.* The council would consist of the clients with whom you have built the most solid relationships. Invite them to have lunch with you from time to time in order to ask them what you're doing right, and in which areas you can improve. They will appreciate being recognized as your special clients, value your enthusiasm in providing them premium service and will typically be more than willing to give you honest feedback and suggestions. It's a way for you to close the back door, to cement your good relationship with them.

[s] *Evaluation forms.* You can develop a service evaluation form to send to all your clients. This would serve the same purpose as your client council, but on a much broader scale. Again, showing that you're constantly striving to do the best for your clients will enhance the ongoing confidence they have in doing business with you. You can request that your clients fill it out anonymously or that they sign their names to it.

Glenda Kemple of Quest Capital Management, previously mentioned in Strategy 84, has developed an evaluation questionnaire for use with all of Quest Capital's clients. Quest Capital's planners take each client to lunch to discuss the evaluation (the questionnaires are sent to the client ahead of time). The questionnaire serves two important purposes: It keeps Quest Capital in touch with its clients' needs and concerns, improving overall client retention, and it provides a formal way to let the clients know that the firm seeks referrals. The form contains a series of questions concerning the quality of service provided by the firm in areas that include the cordiality, politeness and responsiveness of the staff; length of time spent on planning (e.g., is it too short or too long?); and additional services not provided, which the client would like to see. One of the questions asks "Would you feel comfortable introducing our services to your friends and acquaintances?" The next item on the evaluation form simply states, "If so, please list those names below," followed by several blanks for writing in the names of referrals.

[s] *Advisory boards.* Create a board of advisers for your business. This is a technique that has proven market appeal. Your board will advise you on business-related matters, including changing market needs, concerns and value perceptions, which will allow you to improve on the services you provide. If you select board members who have recognized names within the community, your clients and prospects will be impressed. The board members can consist of existing clients, friends, relatives, related professionals (e.g., attorneys and accountants) or even potential clients. If you ask nonclients to sit on the board, they may feel flattered at having been selected and, if they agree, chances are good that they will become your clients anyway!

[s] *Follow-up questionnaires.* After you've completed your assignment for a client, send him or her a questionnaire asking for impressions of the results, your service, your support staff, etc., and for suggestions on ways to improve. Perhaps you should also send a specially prepared questionnaire to those prospects who don't become clients. They might give you some valuable insight, and the concern and sincerity that you demonstrate might very well encourage them to call on you at some later date. (Some even call immediately because they get a new perspective on your professionalism.)

89 ASK ANOTHER PROFESSIONAL TO CRITIQUE YOUR WORK

Send an example of one of your client work sheets or financial plans or portfolio recommendations to another professional in your field. You could also send an audiocassette of a client interview or seminar for evaluation. Only another professional will be able to clearly see and evaluate your strengths and weaknesses. Encourage the other professional to be honest with you in the evaluation. Offer to do the same in return.

RUNNING A LEAN OPERATION

90   ECONOMIZE

Merging with another financial practitioner or firm can create substantial operating efficiencies through sharing office equipment and support staff. You don't have to merge officially; you can continue to maintain your own business identity, but just share support services with the other firm. Having other professionals in the same office suite offers another advantage as well—providing you with intellectual stimulation and shared insight into common problems.

[s] *Making your computer the workhorse it's supposed to be.* If you don't have a computer yet, you need to buy one. For number crunching, word processing, data base operations and desktop publishing, a computer can create efficiencies you never dreamed were possible, saving significant time and payroll dollars. Hire people who are computer literate to help you streamline and enhance your computer-related operations. Of course, unless you're running a large organization, you should learn how to use the computer yourself so that you don't become dependent on any one employee.

91 DEVELOP A GOOD SUPPORT STAFF

Your time is your most valuable commodity, and you should use it in ways that will maximize your profit potential. The best way that you can spend your time is by providing the high-quality service your clients deserve and by promoting and marketing those first-rate services to new potential clients. If you find you spend much time in other ways, you're not making the most out of your own abilities; in other words, you may very well be wasting your time.

⑤ *Hiring an assistant.* You need to be able to delegate responsibility to someone you trust. Hire someone you think will be appropriate, and don't be afraid to grill that person during the initial interview. Don't promise the candidate a rose garden; tell it exactly the way it is. Just be sure to hire someone who can be your alter ego when you need one. A good technique is to tie that person's compensation to your own (i.e., to your business's net profit); it will get him or her focused in the right direction.

⑤ *Hiring a paraprofessional.* Similar to paralegals, these are individuals who want to learn your business, but who haven't had the experience or educational background to set themselves up on their own. Having a paraprofessional in your office can be a tremendous asset.

FOLLOWING THE 80/20 RULE

---

92   MAKE YOUR CLIENTS FEEL SPECIAL

You just can't do too much for your top 20 percent. Give them your "gold" service, just like credit card companies do. Letting them know how special they are will make them appreciate you more. In fact, one professional we heard about actually sends his clients a special gold card he has produced for them.

[S] *Private telephone lines.* Think about getting a separate phone number for those clients and telling them about it in a personalized letter. The number could be a direct line to you. Or it could simply be a number that would always be picked up after, say, the second ring. And, after hours, it should be connected to an answering machine that would ensure a next-day call-back.

Alternatively, you can designate a special time during the day when you'll only take their calls. Let them know that you'll be available just for them every day during an appointed hour. Some professionals even offer their home phone number (and sometimes that of key staff members) as well.

[S] *Rapid response guarantee.* Guarantee a one-hour response to your top clients by someone in your office. If you're busy when a special client calls, your assistant can call the client back and say that you'll be able to get back to him or her within some designated period of time; in the meantime, is there anything the assistant can do for the client? Often, the request or problem is something that can be easily taken care of without your help anyway.

93   WEED OUT THE CLIENTS WHO DON'T FALL WITHIN YOUR PRIMARY TARGET MARKETING GUIDELINES

It sounds like a cold strategy, and perhaps it is. But you have to remember that time is money. Remember who it is that you want additional referrals from: Is it the salesperson earning $35,000 a year who asks you to help make a $2,000 IRA decision every year, or is it the corporate executive who brings in an annual salary of $200,000?

Eliminating or referring out some of your low-productivity clients will enable you to spend more time either working with your top 20 percent or marketing to those prospects who could be among the top 20 percent. Rather than simply abandoning low-productivity clients, however, you should strive to direct them to other professionals who would be able to serve them better and who would value the new clients. You might be able to form a loose association with another professional, newer to the business, who would be eager to take on the clients you're letting go; you could, perhaps, even collect a referral fee for them if it's legal in your state to do so.

---

94 Don't Underprice Your Services

Simple arithmetic will show you why you shouldn't underprice your services. Assuming that each year contains 240 potentially productive workdays, if you spent an average of three and one-half days per client over the course of a year, and each client generated $2,000 in fees, 50 clients would create $100,000 in fee income for your business, leaving you with 65 days—27 percent of your time—for marketing. These extra days represent the *potential* to earn an additional $37,000 in fee income based on ultimately filling them with client service activities.

If, on the other hand, the same 50 clients who generated the same fees each required *four and one-half* days of your time during the year, you would still earn $100,000 in fee income, but you would only have 15 days, or 6 percent of your time, left for marketing—representing the potential for only $6,000 in additional income.

For this reason, it's critical that you consider not only the gross revenue you earn, but the revenue you earn per hour or day and how that relates to your marketing time. To do this, many professionals are keeping records of their time spent with clients and are requiring that their staffs do the same.

50 Clients Generating a Total of $100,000/Year in Fee Income
(Assumes 240 potential working days per year)

Days required per year for client service	Days remaining per year for marketing	Potential additional revenue based on marketing days remaining
3.5	65	$37,000
4.5	15	$ 6,000

You should price your services first according to the value you deliver but also based on how much time you invest with your clients. Depending on your specific income goals, the higher you're able to price your services or the more efficiently you become at delivering them, the fewer clients you'll need and the more free time you'll have for marketing your services. If, at some point, you find that you're acquiring too many clients, try raising your fees or referring out your lowest-producing clients to free up more of your time.

PROFESSIONAL DEVELOPMENT

---

95   Learn How To Become an Active Listener

Some people believe that this is the single most important element in building successful business and personal relationships. Master the principles of active listening and learn how to use them with your clients and prospects. It's critical that you understand what your clients' concerns and goals are and can help reflect and clarify issues for them. For instance, if it were only a matter of facts and numbers, a good computer software program would be enough to produce a stock selection, an insurance program, or a financial plan. And even periodicals such as *Money* magazine provide supplementary information on where and how to buy investments. But only *you* can personalize the service to meet the unique needs and objectives of your client.

Take a course in active listening and communication to further refine your ability to interpret body language, tone of voice and facial expression. Many people say that taking a course like this has been among the most important professional investments they made. In the same vein, develop the knack of asking open-ended rather than "yes/no" questions.

Here are the four keys to active listening:

1. *Understand first; be understood second.* Don't think about making a quick response to your clients' questions; write your thoughts down instead while you carefully listen to what they say.
2. *Restate without repeating.* Think about what your clients are saying and how to paraphrase it so that they know you understand them. Look them in the eye to show that you're focused on them. You can restate their points using such openers as:

   - "Let me see if I understand what you mean..."
   - "In other words, you feel..."
   - "Just to make sure we're on the same wavelength, let me restate what I heard..."
   - "What I hear you saying is..."

Always be sure to ask if the rephrasing is accurate, and give them ample opportunity to respond. With a bit of practice you'll be amazed at the depth of rapport you'll build by using this valuable communication style.

3. *Evaluate without judging.* Ask questions rather than give answers. When your clients make a point, ask questions that allow them to elaborate, giving you more information for your analysis and showing them that you're really listening. Be careful not to interrupt or show boredom.

4. *Pay attention to nonverbal clues.* You can tell whether a person is relaxed or nervous, angry or unhappy through close observation of body language. Paying attention to nonverbal clues can help you understand some of the less obvious messages your clients may be sending you.

STRATEGY

96 STUDY YOUR PRESENTATION SKILLS

Devote some of your off-time to enhancing your one-on-one presentation skills, as well as your techniques in making presentations to a group. After every sales presentation, take one minute to think about it, to evaluate whether it was successful or not and why. But be honest. Committing to this simple process can help you refine your technique and ability to close a sale.

⑤ *Listening to your own audiocassettes.* It might be a painful experience, but very worthwhile as it will enable you to improve on your own speaking ability. Most of us just don't know how we sound to an audience. Trade audiotapes with another professional and exchange critiques of them.

⑤ *Taking a public speaking course.* This can have a dramatic effect on the quality of your seminars and meeting presentations. Many different organizations offer public speaking courses, workshops or private instruction, including Toastmasters and Dale Carnegie Training. Make sure that you take a course that not only shows you the rules in speaking but allows you room to grow. Co-author Alan Parisse offers a specialized program several times a year. Professional trainers often use videos too, a valuable tool to aid learning.

⑤ *Taking an expository writing course.* Writing is a tool that demands regular sharpening. Even the best writers require analytical feedback and careful editing to help them eliminate the kinks in structure, syntax, semantics and grammar that often crop up and detract from or obscure otherwise incisive prose. Many local junior and community colleges offer evening writing courses in basic or advanced composition or in advertising, marketing or journalism that can help you improve and refine your writing skills and get a lot more mileage out of the written material (newsletters, articles, brochures, case studies, ads and even letters) that you provide your target market.

STRATEGY

97 SEEK OUT OTHER PROFESSIONALS AND PROFESSIONAL SERVICES

The other person could be another practitioner with a specialty that would complement yours. Or you could form a loose association with a firm in a related field. It's important that you're not isolated from other professionals and innovative, intellectually stimulating ideas.

⑤ *Listening to what market experts are saying.* Watch "Moneyline," "Wall Street Week" and other financial programs and read reputable financial publications to stay tuned to the views and perceptions of industry experts. On a daily basis, brokers can call various services for stock updates. Pay attention to mutual fund listings to track and evaluate the leading management companies and individual fund ratings.

⑤ *Augmenting your education.* This idea is almost too obvious to state, but almost all the best professionals across the country endorse the importance of ongoing education by taking courses themselves from time to time on tax changes, topics in law or economics to stay abreast of what's happening in the world. They also take advantage of professional organizations and their publications, as well as consumer and trade business journals, to keep up to date.

Most of all, they keep an open mind to new possibilities in their fields of expertise so that they're always offering their clients up-to-the-minute information and the best financial advice. Their educational pursuits help set them apart from the pack.

⑤ *Attending industry conventions.* To optimize your time and get the most mileage from conferences and conventions, you should do the following:

- In advance, list your specific goals and objectives for attending.
- In advance, identify the people you want to meet. If you want to meet a major speaker, for instance, you can often arrange a

15-minute "coffee meeting" before or after the talk by writing or calling in advance.
- In advance, map out your convention schedule.
- Prepare for post-convention P.R. Do a press release, if appropriate.
- Contact your clients to share the new ideas and information you obtained (through a meeting, phone call, letter, special-edition newsletter, audiocassette, etc.)

⑤ *Sharing due-diligence responsibilities.* If you're a financial planner, this is a particularly effective way to save time as well as to benefit from the insights of other professionals. Set up a regular monthly meeting with a group of other planners to exchange ideas and information on topics of interest, including current economic issues and new product opportunities. It will make your life simpler and at the same time enable you to offer better service to your clients.

Work with the group to develop other time-saving ideas. If you have an independent practice, you can set up a marketing "think tank" consisting of stockbrokers, insurance agents, financial planners and other professionals to meet periodically and exchange marketing ideas.

STRATEGY

98 MAKE THAT FIRST IMPRESSION A GOOD ONE

Let's face it. You're never judged exclusively on the merit of what you do or how well you do it; you're also judged on the way you present yourself to the world. Show your professionalism through your personal appearance as well as through your professional skills. You want to draw your prospects to you, so project the image that you're successful, busy and that it's hard to get in the door. To be successful you have to look successful. You should dress to appeal to your market.

MANAGING YOUR TIME

STRATEGY

99   GET A CELLULAR PHONE

How much time do you spend driving around during an average day?
Unless you're listening to educational tapes or dictating memos or letters into a tape recorder, all of that driving time is probably being
wasted. You could be using it instead to make calls to your clients or
calls on their behalf. Cellular phones aren't "out of reach" anymore,
so you might very well consider getting one. And recent advances in
telecommunications technology have made portable phones equally
advantageous to own: You can always have personal access to a telephone; you don't ever have to be out of touch with your business associates or clients; you can always be "on call." Some people are
reluctant to use cellular phones because they fear that, if they do,
they'll never be able to be free from office interruptions. This objec-
tion merits two different observations. First, part of making a service
valuable to the market involves being available to it. Second, many
professionals who use cellular phones claim that it is actually relaxing
and often anxiety-reducing to have telephone access while driving.

STRATEGY

100   KEEP YOUR OWN CALENDAR

How many times have you had an appointment set for you that was a time-waster? Your time is precious, and you, rather than your secretary or assistant, should be the person allocating it. You can tell your secretary which clients and other business associates you'll make time to meet. You should also screen requests for suppliers and vendors who want to see you. This, in fact, is an excellent area in which you can delegate responsibility; have your secretary or assistant see them.

101   TRACK YOUR MARKETING EFFORTS

Keep track of the time and money you spend on the various marketing tools and ideas that you test. To the extent that you do this, you can get a sense of which ones have been the most cost-effective and how you can fine-tune them to get even better results in the future.

Conclusion

You'll find that you can implement most of the ideas we've presented in this book quickly and easily, without making any fundamental changes to your business, and with minimal planning time. Each of the ideas has worked very well on its own for someone. If you're satisfied with the way your business is going and perhaps only want to augment your client base, just use those ideas that will help you accomplish that goal.

But maybe you're not satisfied with the progress of your business. Perhaps you feel that your income isn't high enough, or your clients don't stick with you, or you can't seem to find enough time to serve them well. If you'd like to see an overall change in your business performance, revamping your marketing approach in each of the major areas we've covered can help you succeed.

Make a pact with yourself to enhance your business in each of these areas—targeting your market, developing a data base, connecting with your market and using external and internal marketing strategies—to initiate and deliver a high level of service. Many of the ideas will work well for you, as they have for the professionals who conceived them, but only if you make the commitment to try them out.

Try to resist the temptation to procrastinate. The following techniques may help:

- Try the "salami technique": Rebuilding your business may seem like a formidable task, but if you slice it into small pieces you can attack one at a time.

- Adopt a five-minute plan: See how much you can get done in just five minutes toward listing the steps needed to implement an idea; then quit. Maybe you'll feel motivated to continue. If not, you'll at least be further along than you were before.
- Use the worst-first system: Do the worst task first. The rest of the project will seem that much easier.
- Go public: Announce your intentions to others. It will then be harder for you to back down.

Choose any 12 of these 101 Power Strategies and plan to try one a month for the next 12 months. If one idea works well, you'll be well motivated to go on to the next. And if it doesn't work well, go on to the next one anyway; chances are, if one idea doesn't get optimal results for you, another one will, and in most cases they will have a cumulative effect. It often takes a while for marketing momentum to build, and you must be persistent to achieve good results. The extra time and energy you spend implementing new ideas will be the basis for making you *better* and unique.

Successful people are successful because they do what others won't do and because they work hard to achieve the results that they want. There's an old aphorism that says "Luck comes to those with calloused hands." So does prosperity.

The ultimate objective of a good marketing plan is to get your prospects to call you and ask if you have time to see them. Remember, your goal isn't to sell, but to let your prospects buy.

Although all the ideas in this book are tried and true, we tried to keep them concise and general enough that they could be widely adapted for varying use. If you find that one in particular works especially well, or if one jogged your creativity and sparked a new idea, or if you just have an interesting concept that we failed to include, please write to us and let us know.

Dick Wollack   Alan Parisse
Liquidity Fund   Alan J. Parisse & Associates
1900 Powell Street   1630 30th Street, Suite 304
Emeryville, CA 94608   Boulder, CO 80301-1014

POWER MARKETING STRATEGY CONTRIBUTORS

Chapter 1: Targeting Your Market

Strategy 2:
Targeting by financial status—the power of political association: Joseph C. Bowers, Financial Advisory Network, Radnor, Pennsylvania

Strategy 3:
Targeting by gender—divorce planning for women: Kathleen Muldoon, Carter Financial Management, Dallas, Texas

Strategy 4:
' **Small, successful businesses:** Lewis Walker, CFP, Walker Capital Management Corporation, Atlanta, Georgia
Targeting CPAs: Joe Foss, Foss & Company, San Francisco, California

Strategy 5:
Financial planning for corporate employees: Richard D. Curb, IDS Financial Services, Austin, Texas

Strategy 6:
Targeting by product specialty: Greg Schasiepen, GRS Financial Services, Mountain View, California

Chapter 2: Developing a Data Base of Prospects

Strategy 8:
Registered voters—names from the wealthiest voting precincts: Eugene L. Naegele, CFP, Investment Management & Research, Tucson, Arizona
Retired/retiring school teachers—public school board minutes: Stephen M. Geraghty, Educators Financial Services, Los Gatos, California
Parents of college-bound children—elementary school directories: Donald M. Finsthwait, Stanford Investment Group, Palo Alto, California

Strategy 9:
Chambers of Commerce New business listings: Norman Boone, Salient Financial, San Francisco, California
Attending chambers of commerce meetings: Dan Adams, Adams Financial Services, Dubuque, Iowa

Strategy 10:
Insider trading reports: Fay F. Jones, Protected Investors of America, Menlo Park, California

Business opportunities section of *The Wall Street Journal:* John R. Austin, San Francisco, California
Real estate transaction notices: D'Anne Brownell, First Pacific Financial Services, Solvang, California
Divorce notices: Philip R. Walters, Walters Financial Corporation, Orlando, Florida

Strategy 11:
Alumni news: Susan E. Arbuckle, Pennsylvania Financial Group, Inc., Columbia, Maryland

Strategy 12:
Twofers: Kevin D. Seacat, Titan Capital Corporation, Mesa, Arizona
Over-30 baseball club: John Coffey, Financial Investment Analysts, Carnegie, Pennsylvania
Free dinner-for-two drawings: T.R. Metzger, First Financial Group of Illinois, Belleville, Illinois

Strategy 13:
Sharing leads through swap meets: Judith G. Benbow, IDS American Express, Auburn, California; and Altair M. Gobo, Financial Advisory Centre, Wayne, New Jersey

Strategy 15:
Free directory listings: Don Reid, Integrity Financial, Los Angeles, California

Strategy 16:
Starting at the top—calling on top executives: Thomas P. Marth, The Mass Mutual, Las Vegas, Nevada

Chapter 4: Seminars and Special Events

Strategy 22:
Seminars on current financial topics: Douglas Obey, Dedham, Massachusetts
Seminars on health care insurance: Wayne Watson, Investacorp, Denver, Colorado
Planning for college—Seminars for day-care parents: Eric G. Suhr, R.G. Toppins & Company, Walnut Creek, California
Videotaped presentations on repositioning assets: Robert C. Monin, CFP, Progressive Planning Services, Williamsville, New York
Financial services seminars for the newly widowed: Lynn Van Buren, CMP Financial Services, Chicago, Illinois
Retirement planning for temporary office workers: David Folkerson, Foresight Financial Planning, Salt Lake City, Utah

Free seminars to businesses and associations: Joseph C. Dekat,
Financial Planning Partners, Mission, Kansas
Availability as a fill-in speaker: Robert A. Crecelius, Sr., Wealth
Concepts, Princeton, Indiana
Seminars on tax-advantaged investments: Stephen S. Hall, CFP,
Retirement Planning Services, Knoxville, Tennessee
**Savings and retirement planning for the self-employed—presentations at
real estate salespersons' meetings:** James J. Hagel, CFP, Financial
Consultants of Michigan, Holland, Michigan

Strategy 25:
Seminars in translation: James Burke, J.D., CFP, Campbell, California

Strategy 28:
Seminar weekend "getaways": Randall T. Stewart, Integrated Resources
Equity Corporation, Buffalo Grove, Illinois

Strategy 30:
Illustrating the message—Hershey™ bar giveaways: Stephen J. Hart,
Investment Centers of America, Hazen, North Dakota

Strategy 31:
Using humor: Philip Hartwell, Hartwell Financial Services, Torrance,
California

Strategy 35:
Prepackaged seminars: Aubrey Morrow, Financial Designs, San Diego,
California

Strategy 36:
Offering your services as an adult educator: Lawrence D. Doff, Real
Pro, Annandale, Virginia

Strategy 36:
Getting into the lecture circuit—using P.R. firms: Jason H. Kurchner,
Kurchner, Vahanian, Martin & Co., Saratoga Springs, New York

Strategy 37:
"Payday" picnics: Johannes Fure, Fure Financial Corporation, Eden
Prairie, Minnesota
Barbecues for clients: Robert B. Anderson, Capital Planning Group,
Paradise, California
Inviting wholesalers: Karen Thyssen, Watermark Financial Services,
Appleton, Wisconsin
Parties: Doug Hesse, Hesse Financial Advisors, Roswell, Georgia
Free mutual fund drawings: Frank D. Olesuk, Frank D. Olesuk
Financial Services, Crystal Lake, Illinois

Blood drives: Charles Scarborough, IDS Financial Services, Austin, Texas

Chapter 5: Marketing Media You Create on Your Own

Strategy 38:
$100 bills: Sidney Friedman, Corporate Financial Services, Philadelphia, Pennsylvania
Unsigned checks: Richard Kado, Edmonds, Washington
Three-minute egg timers: Robert Mark, Jonathan Alan & Company, White Plains, New York
Candy: Kevin Coyle, Consulting Research, Northfield, Illinois
Promoting something that's free: T. Battaglia, Allegheny Investments, Pittsburgh, Pennsylvania
The "drip method": Phil Broyles, Broyles Management Company, San Francisco, California
Last-ditch drips—letters/questionnaires: C. Bradshaw Davis, CIGNA Financial Services Co., San Diego, California

Strategy 46:
Tip from the top: Allan Feldman, CFP, Total Services, Scottsdale, Arizona

Strategy 48:
Videos illustrating investment opportunities: Jares Financial Group, Minneapolis, Minnesota

Strategy 49:
Videotapes for personal marketing: Bill Palmer, Runkel & Palmer, Diamond Bar, California

Strategy 51:
Nicknames: Barry "Bear" Friedlander, RE/MAX, Boulder, Colorado

Strategy 54:
Making it personal: Gregory A. Kelleher, Stafford Springs, Connecticut
Including a keepsake in the flier: Dennis De Young, GBS Financial Corporation, Sherman Oaks, California

Strategy 56:
Thanksgiving cards: Barbara DiPalma, Spring Valley, New York
Graphic illustrations of investment products: Robert H. Coe, Cowen & Company, Boston, Massachusetts
Letters to newborn children: W. Douglas O'Rear, Chubb Securities Corporation, Brentwood, Tennessee

Letters to seminar attendees: James N. Reardon, J.D., CFP, Clayton Financial Services, Inc., Topeka, Kansas

Strategy 57:
Neighborhood newsletters: Kristie Minkoff, IREC, Wilsonville, Oregon

Strategy 58:
Using other companies' newsletters: Thomas E. Seifert, Prudential Bache Securities, Scottsdale, Arizona

Strategy 60:
Including an information request coupon: Peter R. Wheeler, Financial Services, San Diego, California
Sending newsletters to other professionals: Donald J. Best, Jr., Partners in Financial Planning, Denver, Colorado

Chapter 6: Advertising and Public Relations

Strategy 61:
Testimonial ads: Mark Negless, Private Ledger Financial Services, Vancouver, Washington

Strategy 62:
Cooperative advertising: Mary Vizioli, Stephens Associates, Denville, New Jersey

Strategy 65:
Newspaper inserts: George Bates, Bates Financial Services, Rockford, Illinois

Strategy 68:
Becoming a quotable source: Ed Gor, Associates in Financial Planning, Houston, Texas
Cable stations: Thomas G. Hinkel, Integrated Planning Group, West Palm Beach, Florida

Strategy 70:
Articles on charitable giving: Stanley H. Shawl, Pacific Southwest Planning Group, Sacramento, California

Chapter 7: Delivering the Service and Obtaining Referrals

Strategy 74:
Serving refreshments: Carol A. Wright, Carol A. Wright & Associates, San Francisco, California
Rolling office: F.J. Hildebrand, Lowry Financial Services Corporation, Seabrook, Texas

Reminder cards: Warren J. Berg, Warren J. Berg & Associates, Green Bay, Wisconsin

Strategy 75:
List of services and products: Burns Landess, Financial Focus Corporation, Memphis, Tennessee

Strategy 76:
Contacting your clients with both good and bad news: Mary Buelow, Triple Check Financial Services, Englewood, Florida
Birthday greetings to clients and clients' families: Dickinson W. Sparks, KMS, Lynnwood, Washington; and Michael Furois, Chesterton State Bank, Chesterton, Indiana

Strategy 77:
Sharing your discoveries: Stuart M. Purcell, CPA, Purcell Wealth Management, San Rafael, California

Strategy 79:
One-dollar gifts: Lee Pennington, Pennington, Bass & Associates, Lubbock, Texas
Gift certificates: Gerald A. Townsend, Townsend Financial Group, Raleigh, North Carolina

Strategy 81:
Billing for referrals: Raymond E. Moore, CLU, ChFC, Chubb Securities Corporation, Richmond, Virginia
Getting referrals up front: Preston S. Caves, PlanVest Advisors, Manhattan Beach, California
Asking who needs the most help: Harry N. Davis, Waddell & Reed, St. Petersburg, Florida
Asking for the names of your clients' competitors: David A. Saltzman, David A. Saltzman & Associates, Miami, Florida
Confiding in clients: Elizabeth Sampson, AFP, Los Angeles, California
An evening of entertainment: Michael J. Ford, Jr., CLU, ChFC, RFP, Ford Financial Corporation, Worthington, Ohio
Thank-you gifts: Jack Prior, Prior Financial Planning, San Diego, California
Referral incentives—hot air balloon rides: John A. Kiriaze, Financial Advisors, La Jolla, California
Saying thanks in a newsletter: Larry Goodrich, IM&R, Bellingham, Washington

Strategy 82:
Planting your business card: Gregory Ryan, Christopher Weil & Company, Fair Oaks, California

Strategy 83:
Doing something extra special so that your clients tell everyone: Charles H. Kuhtz III, Stifel, Nicolaus & Company, Milwaukee, Wisconsin

Strategy 84:
Networking receptions: Glenda Kemple, Quest Capital Management, Dallas, Texas
Giving free seminar tickets to other professionals for their best clients: Mary Rhea, CFP, San Diego, California

Strategy 85:
Someone else's castoffs becoming your clients: Robert E. Brandt, Valparaiso, Indiana

Strategy 86:
Developing a relationship with a mortgage brokerage firm: IREC, Sacramento, California
Developing a relationship with a casualty insurance firm: James J. Hughes, Hughes Financial Management, Newburyport, Massachusetts
Developing a relationship with a discount stock brokerage firm: Tom Dillon, Bruno Stolze & Company, St. Louis, Missouri
Certificates for free service: Michael K. Stein, CFP, Financial Planning & Management, Boulder, Colorado

Chapter 8: Sustaining Your Success

Strategy 88:
Client evaluation forms: Glenda Kemple, Quest Capital Management, Dallas, Texas

Strategy 97:
Listening to what market experts are saying: Thomas E. Seifert, Prudential Bache Securities, Scottsdale, Arizona

Index

NOTE: The names of strategy contributors are italicized.